Servitization

Servitization

Assessment Protocol for Action

Antonio Pérez Márquez

BEP

BUSINESS EXPERT PRESS

Leader in applied, concise business books

Servitization: Assessment Protocol for Action

Cover design by Antonio Pérez Márquez

Interior design by Exeter Premedia Services Private Ltd., Chennai, India

First published in 2022 by
Business Expert Press, LLC
222 East 46th Street, New York, NY 10017
www.businessexpertpress.com

ISBN-13: 978-1-63742-420-9 (paperback)
ISBN-13: 978-1-63742-421-6 (e-book)

Business Expert Press Service Systems and Innovations in Business and Society Collection

First edition: 2022

10 9 8 7 6 5 4 3 2 1

Description

The servitization construct is generally described and accepted as a strategic model of organizational innovation and value co-creation for the manufacturing company through the identification and development of service opportunities.

In this context, the adoption of a servitization strategy is, first of all, a matter of managerial decision and a contingency factor with a high impact on the business model. A process that involves investigating the integrity of the company's value chain to identify and estimate factors and business opportunities for services, determining potential profits and considering contingencies to minimize in terms of costs and risks.

It is a topic of high impact in today's industries and that responds to the permanent contingency of business in highly competitive markets. It is based on the avant-garde scientific knowledge available and on the author's extensive professional and academic experience on the subject, with the purpose of conceptualizing and building a valid referential framework that supports the *learner*[1] in the entrepreneurial initiative of the company and its process of motivation, analysis, and decision to adopt a servitization strategy as a factor for the creation of value and better results.

The practical implication lies in providing a reliable, practical, and effective instrument from the academic and industrial perspective, and its corresponding collateral orientation for the development of the relevant dynamic managerial capability for motivation and adoption decision.

Keywords

servitization; service; value chain; business integral value chain; service compliance; dynamic capabilities; innovation; sustainability

---

[1] Manufacturing industry executives and managers, professionals interested in the service business, professors and university students, researchers, consulting firms and anyone else interested in adding service value to his or her business.

Contents

Testimonials

"This book presents, in a profound and surprising way, how much not only the concepts had evolved, but how the required skills have changed and how to develop them within organizations, starting from the necessary strategic formulation to identify the tools for their evaluation."—**Julio Bucci, Executive President of Pipeline Investment Limited, Bermuda**

*"*Servitization *offers the reader a holistic and practical vision on the subject of the Service in the industrial context that requires great understanding for its implementation."*—**Cesar Bernal, Director of the Innovation and Strategy Research Group, International School of Economic and Administrative Sciences, Universidad de La Sabana, Bogotá, Colombia**

"In his new concise, expert book Servitization: Assessment Protocol for Action, *author Antonio Pérez Márquez provides the necessary practical foundations and inspirational insights to allow readers to develop, deploy, maintain, and continuously innovate a service strategy for a business, non-profit, and even an individual's life."*—**Jim Spohrer, Board Member, International Society of Service Innovation Professionals**

Preface

Servitization

The servitization construct is generally described and accepted as a strategic model or process of organizational innovation/transformation of co-creation of value for the business/manufacturing company through the identification and development of service opportunities.

The primary purpose of a company or business is to create prosperity through the generation of solutions and benefits where the greatest component of value addition, and offer to its user/consumer, is in the service.

In this context, the adoption of a servitization strategy in the manufacturing company is, firstly, a matter of managerial decision and a contingency factor with a high impact on the business model. Is it a process that involves investigating the integrity of the company's value chain to identify and estimate factors and business opportunities for services, determining potential profits, and considering contingencies to minimize in terms of costs and risks?

Servitization focuses its action on the transformation of the manufacturing industries by adding the value of the service to its business strategy based on the satisfaction of the end customer, the sustainability of the company, and the competitiveness of the market.

This work is based on the avant-garde scientific knowledge available and on the author's extensive professional and academic experience on the subject, with the purpose of conceptualizing and building a valid referential framework that supports the reader in the entrepreneurial initiative of the company and its process of motivation, analysis, and decision to adopt a servitization strategy as a factor for the creation of value and better results.

The practical implication lies in providing a reliable, sensible, and effective instrument from the academic and industrial perspective to the critical process of conceptualization, modeling, operationalization, implementation, and measurement of a servitization initiative, and in the corresponding collateral orientation for the development of the relevant dynamic managerial capacity for motivation and adoption decision.

Antonio Pérez Márquez

Acknowledgments

I want to first express my gratitude to the ISSIP in its promoters and series editor, Jim Spohrer, for providing the opportunity to all service innovation professionals to offer their knowledge and experiences about service through a book. Likewise, I want to thank my lovely wife, Miriam Celina García, who has lived with me and shared the magnificent experience of many years studying, teaching, and practicing service science in business and entrepreneurship environments.

My thanks also go to my colleagues and friends from the Academy and Industry for their review and enriching comments on the draft of this work, respectively: Professor Cesar Augusto Bernal, director of the research group on innovation and strategy at the International School of Economic and Administrative Sciences of the University of La Sabana in Bogotá, Colombia, and Dr. Julio Bucci, with extensive managerial experience in the Latin American oil industry and current CEO of pipelines business of the private company that serves the Colombian oil and gas industry.

I also want to thank the universities and their authorities who have allowed the academic inclusion of the service approach through their executive courses, workshops, advanced diplomas, and consulting services to companies.

Lastly, I want to thank Susan Schmidt-Perez and Ruben Pérez Márquez for their generous support in making a better possible understanding of this work.

Introduction

How to Add Service Value to the Business?

We live in a service economy and society. They permeate the life of the individual and the daily life of society, determine the level of the quality of life and social development, and today constitute the main factor of well-being with a growing trend.

This dimension of services places them in a preeminent position in social interaction and in the economic exchange of society; they contribute two-thirds of the Gross Domestic Product (GDP) of the economic activity of nations, regardless of their level of development. They constitute the largest source of job creation globally and are increasingly consolidating their trend of greater development and social and economic growth.

With this perspective, both organizations and businesses on a global scale are mobilized in unison, driven by constant changes in the dynamics of users/consumers, competition, and markets in the quest to nurture their value chain and strengthen sustainability of one´s proposal by adding or developing the service.

Servitization as a strategic innovative model responds to this organizational and business challenge, placing the company's management in the position of investigating the comprehensiveness of the value chain to identify and estimate factors and service business opportunities, determining potential profits, and considering contingencies to minimize in terms of costs and risks.

The potential beneficiary of this work, such as managers, executives, professionals, entrepreneurs, and university professors as well as students who want to know, how to acquire new skills, refresh, or update knowledge on the subject, will find in this work an orientation tool, brief and practical, of the fundamentals and approaches necessary for the analysis, adoption, and implementation of a servitization strategy.

The work is structured in five chapters with their respective application dynamics that incorporate the reader's own experiences and experiences on the subject. An extract as a referential reading of the issues is discussed. The set of own and added terms on the topics covered is defined and contained in the "Terminology" section at the end of the last chapter. Likewise, the references used occupy a separate place and are structured in a general way and the specific ones corresponding to each chapter.

Chapter 1: *The Service Value Chain* establishes, through Servilogy,[1] a cutting-edge holistic vision and the corresponding theoretical foundation of the service ecosystem as the foundation of the servitization initiative.

Chapter 2: *Servitization: An Assessment Holistic Perspective* describes the structure and the integral valuation process for the adoption of a servitization strategy.

Chapter 3: *Service Compliance Management* focuses on the delivery process, experience, verification, and results of carrying out the service, by describing a connection pattern between the service code of the company's value proposition, the measurement of the delivery (instruments and indicators), and the assurance of the contracted obligation, in accordance with the company's manifest commitment to its user.

Chapter 4 on *Dynamic Capabilities* outlines the skills for the provision and management of services and establishes their differentiating character in relation to the skills required for manufacturing activities. Socioemotional capacities that also turn out to be keys to success and merit their identification, consolidation, or development in manufacturing contexts.

The final chapter *Innovation and Sustainability* develops from the servitization perspective as an innovative business model, two concepts associated with the survival or stability of a company in the market over time: competition and permanence. It shows two schemes to carry out these processes within the framework of the design and continuous renewal of a competitive and continuously growing business model.

---

[1] Study of the principles, concepts, approaches, methods, and instruments of service from the perspective of human action as a reasoned and deliberative behavior.

CHAPTER 1

The Service Value Chain

Servilogy or etymologically, the study of service, is the term used in this work to mean and address here the question of service: principles, concepts, approaches, methods, and instruments from its original foundation in human action as Von Mises[1] points out:

> Human action is purposeful behavior ... Action is will put into operation and transformed into an agency, is aiming at ends and goals, is the ego´s meaningful response to stimuli and to the conditions of its environment, is a person´s conscious adjustment to the state of the universe that determines his life. (Von Mises 1998)

From this anthropocentric conception, Servilogy, based on the axiom of reasoned human action, deals with its contexts capable of causing certain intentional and influenced actions, which differentiate it from Praxeology (study of the logical structure of action "praxis" as such) and other perspectives of simple physical effort or work. The force and factors that drive a human being in a certain way and "by acting, one chooses, determines, and tries to reach an end."[2]

In this context, the service turns out to be the masterpiece of human action and the central theoretical foundation of the servitization construct: an imperative of social welfare and of the appropriate income of the entrepreneurial effort.

Fundamentals of Service

From the service perspective as a reasoned and deliberated organizational action, of impact and advantage for the business activity, what principles, concepts, and approaches should be considered in the creation and development of a servitization strategy?

The outcomes of the research communities[3] in the field of services activity have integrated pioneering, interdisciplinary, and systematic concepts and approaches, and shaped a solid conceptual structure that has evolved into what today has been called Service Science.[4] These postulates make up the foundations that support this servitization proposal.

What Is Service?

The act, performance, or activity of co-creating value. This concept sets distinctive qualities with its collateralities in the scope and performance of organizations: *Inherence, intangibility, interactivity, and purpose*. That is, of an essentially imperceptible and inseparable nature, it creates or develops interaction between entity or entities (relationship) with a reciprocal intention or spirit.

These qualities[5] are contained in an activity, act, operation, process, performance, or experience of particular characteristics that contribute to the identification, conceptualization, and differentiation of a service proposal:

(a) **User participation.**[6] User involvement impacts the conception, provision, and management of the service. It is the *raison d'être* of a service. It is an experience that the user lives in the service encounter and environment where it is a leading part of the interaction and the outcome. This user experience shapes its perception and impresses in a positive, negative, or neutral way the provision of the service and, in general, the performance of the system. The difference or gap between the service proposal and its fulfillment determines or not the user's satisfaction and, consequently, the success of the undertaking or business.

(b) **Intangibility.** The immaterial nature of the service of not being physically perceived places it in the field of ideas and experiences with considerable implications for its provision, management, and marketing: design, valuation, differentiation, promotion, patenting, and sampling. It is the central differentiator between a consumer goods company and a service company. The act of selling intangible poses new challenges.

(c) **Heterogeneity.** The heterogeneous nature of the service or a mixture of various intervening factors is related not only to the service itself but to the human factor that makes it depend on who, how, when, and where it is provided. Its impact on delivery and management permeates quality (excellence), user satisfaction, and organizational performance.

(d) **Simultaneity (Inseparability).** The interaction of the service is inseparable. The action of provision and use or utilization is simultaneous. In other words, they are experiences whose quality of being memorable requires from the provider a *dynamic performance capability* of zero defects.

(e) **Perishability.** The simultaneity between provision and use gives the service a perishable character that results in the impossibility of its conservation, storage, or inventory. This implies a company strategic challenge in managing the capacity variability and demand.

(f) **Absence of property.** The service (intangible), unlike a product (tangible), only gives the right to access a specific use of it or receive a specific benefit. In other words, it does not involve the transfer of property; it is only conceived in the *memorable part of the lived experience*. The business challenge and success of the service proposal lie in the strategic understanding of the customer experience as a key differentiating factor and in the management of integrating and sharing resources with and between users.

These service natural conditions, strategically considered, serve to the *service criticality* to adjust and give stability to the company's capacity in the demand-supply relationship in a dynamic environment:

- Service is an intangible and nontransferable personal experience.
- The service is simultaneously provided and used.
- Service capacity is a perishable *commodity*.
- The service natural cyclical variation creates active (peaks) and passive (empty) periods.

It should be noted that it may be ambitious to assume that there is a definition that covers all aspects of service, and consequently, a generally accepted concept that should be equally applicable to all kinds of service organizations. However, the term service is polysemic in nature and gives it "unilaterality or uniformity" aspects that significantly affect the delivery process and must be previously considered. In this sense, each service must be evaluated by applying certain criteria. Roger Schmenner in the "Service Process Matrix"[7] proposes two dimensions that are pertinent to consider for this purpose: the effort degree of intensity and the degree of interaction and personalization. This aspect will be dealt with in greater breadth and depth later in the section's service taxonomy: The service ecosystem.

The Service Scope

The *service space* is shaped and based on three pillars:

1. **The personal, volunteering, or altruistic service** conceived as "the action of freely giving and accepting to satisfy human needs, which results in the common benefit."[8]

   This person-to-person or face-to-face service encounter not only means the interaction between two people but also involves a more complex context with essential implications for the design of the service proposal. It involves the absolute or relative proportion of the physical-emotional interference, of interpersonal interaction, and intensity of the required information.

   Personal service is the source where genuine and innovative behavior and performance are nurtured, which makes possible the differentiating culture of prestige, growth, and social and entrepreneurial benefits.[9]

   On this pillar, the scaffolding of what is known today as the service ecosystem is configured and the details of which the reader will know while reading it.

2. **The public or collaborative service** is defined here as the activities reserved, provided and delegated by the public administration as required by law to respond to the performance of society. Likewise, collaborative interaction between citizens, communities, and "nongovernmental organizations" with a social spirit that contributes to the welfare state, the cost of which is borne by the taxpayers. It should be clarified that the private companies by delegation that

participate in the public service do not receive an economic compensation higher (profitability) than the amount invested or its provision cost and maintenance. This service, as it is a matter of public interest, will always be supervised by the state.

The public service is exemplified by well-known services such as health, order and security, legal issues, education, transportation, drinking water supply, military, and so on.

In this context, a service proposal to meet the needs and expectations of this collaborative sector requires the common and particular considerations of this activity. Here, the personal attitude and contribution and the social marketing focus are remarkable.

3. **Private or exchange service.** The one provided for profit or valuable consideration by delegated private or public companies and corporations for the purpose of satisfying particular needs and expectations.

The *Customer Service* and *Service Management,* as it is generally known, is inherent to the organization, company, or business. Its offer and provision constitute a form or strategy of identification and prestige in the market, as well as utility and business growth. In this environment, customer service is a two-way action by targeting the external customer (user) and the internal customer (employee) with decisive implications for their management, delivery, and compliance.

The research community of the emerging Science of Service conceptualizes it as the action of value co-creation. That is, the interaction that serves the purpose of creating shared value as the basis for satisfying the user's expectant need and the opportunity to develop an individual, effective, consistent, profitable, and long-term relationship that ensures the sustainability of the company.

The servitization construct is founded on this pillar.

The Service Modality

The service is bimodal or dual, that is, it is manifested and delivered under two modalities:

1. **Face-to-face, physical, or traditional.** It corresponds to the physical space and interaction of value co-creation where the moment of

truth occurs: the user's encounter with the service. The management of this encounter, by considering their own and unique aspects, impacts its result with the collateral implications.

This people interaction, in person or by phone, has an altruistic and collaborative exchange or consideration purpose, as well as its management as the act of infusing, directing, and coordinating the actions of people and resources to provide answers or agile and timely solutions to users. They have been mainly the scope and study objective of the Service Management discipline, today known as the Service Science, until the advent of the Internet.

2. **Virtual.** It refers to the online, digital, or electronic service offered and provided through the network, using information and communication technologies (ICT). This modality significantly broadens the horizon of the service and contributes to scaling the level of quality and its management. The Information Technology Infrastructure Library or ITIL, its acronym in English, as well as known technological developments (ISO/IEC 20000, COBIT, Smart Service Management, among others.) offer detailed descriptions of an extensive set of management procedures designed not only to help organizations achieve quality and efficiency in their operations (ERP, CRM) but to expand the range of services offered through the Internet such as Business to Business (B2B for its acronym in English), Business to Consumer (B2C), Client to Client, Peer Network (C2C, P2P), and so forth.

The Service Systematic and Transversal

The service has its own way of working. The service itself is systemic due to its integrating nature of resources that together contribute to a common purpose. The service system or work system supports the value-creation process. In this environment, it forms what is known as a service system or *service package*[10] and is defined as the integration, configuration, and dynamic alignment of resources of various kinds (human, financial, technological, infrastructure, information, etc.) with the purpose of creating shared value.

The co-creation of value emerges from the interaction of many parts that can be formalized, analyzed, and designed despite its complexity.[11]

The relationship between the system parts is such that each part operation affects the system as an all. In this context, problem-solving must be seen in an integrated way, making use of systemic thinking. In the service realm, this turns out to be a critical factor to consider.

Likewise, the service has an original quality as an entity and reasoned act that gives it a universal character by being present in all areas and disciplines of all human-social activity: transversality. Considered as a person soft skill, it constitutes a potential factor for the company to expand its resource base. This dynamic capability will be developed in detail in Chapter 4.

The service system is configured by four stages or overlapping phases that interact, create value, and facilitate innovation in the different contexts of the service. These are as follows:

1. **Service design.** The process of creation and development, comprehensive and effective, of the service proposal. It is the holistic vision of the value-creation interaction in the user experience. The business outcomes are based on the knowledge and human and social behavior of the users.

    On what factors is a service devised and tailor-made?[12]

    (a) **User.** Focused on and from the user's perspective. The results of qualitative research, the market audit, the database techniques, and business analytics allow for the inquiry and knowledge of the user/customer, undoubtedly, facilitate the strategic business decision-making, and are decisive in the effective design of a service value proposition.

    The concept of the user profile, focused on the knowledge and understanding of the user's needs and expectations, is the central focus of attention in the design of any type of distinctive and effective service proposal. However, this concept of user profile is still standard and is served by the concept of market segmentation, although it leads to the final conception of the individual user, overcoming personalization and giving rise to the future singularization (customization) of the proposal of service.

    (b) **Co-creation.** Identify and integrate all the actors involved in the service design. These are all the groups and factors of interest in the service: customers, employees, suppliers, referents, and influencers.

(c) **Composition.** Sections in sequence, the phases, and processes that make up the service experience. Diagrams, maps, or workflows are valid and valuable application tools for this activity.

(d) **Tangibility.** It incorporates experiences that make perception, understanding, and trust in service possible.

(e) **Holistic character**. It incorporates all points of contact and perspectives from the user experience and their interactions to generate outcomes.

2. **Engineering and architecture of service.** It is the application of the knowledge generated by science for the value creation and the construction of the capacity to provide the service: *personnel* (with mentality and culture), *operations* (processes, procedures, mechanisms, diagrams, maps), *architecture* (physical infrastructure and technology), and *marketing* (image and communication management). It translates the user needs and expectations into the language of the company.

It is the strategic vision of the service space, purpose, and competitive environment that originates from a user with identified and unsatisfied needs that is executed through an implementation process. This strategic process has evolved from being transactional in nature to being relational based on user experience.

3. **Service delivery.** It is the integral and specific process of interaction, provision, and assurance of the appropriate service use.

What elements to consider in an encounter and service delivery?

(a) **The actors and associates.** All those involved in the service provision (customers, employees, suppliers, referents, and influencers).

(b) **The external environment (physical)** where the user receives the service and the internal environment (culture) influenced by the beliefs and values of the organizational actors that give meaning to the activity and guide their behavior in it.

(c) **The process.** The set of successive tasks, activities, or operations carried out for the delivery of the service.

(d) **The value promise.** The organizational method or the characteristic and differentiating formula that the company uses to deliver the service and that has the value for the user/customer when satisfying their expectations.

(e) **Image and communication management.** Dimensions that contribute to the user perception of quality and give transcendence to the service.

4. **Compliance management.** It is the management of the process of delivery, reception, measurement of the evolution, the achievement of the purpose, and the result of the performance of the service in accordance with its design. Later, in chapter 3 of this proposal, the critical phases of this strategic process are detailed, and advanced measurement schemes and instruments are presented, aligned with the user, the process management and the business, such as quality (excellence), user interaction, experience, satisfaction, relationship, and trust.

The Service Ecosystem

What Is It?

Taken from biology, the term ecosystem generally refers to a community of actors (individuals, organizations, and institutions) that interact and affect each other through their activities based on their purposes and environments involved.[13]

In the evolution of the service concept from the encounter/interaction and the ambit where it takes place, the service ecosystem is the set of entities that act in domain-specific roles as providers and users of services of available services that enable community interaction and co-creation and the appropriate architecture for engineering, delivery, and governance.

It is also considered as "a relatively autonomous and self-adjusting system of actors that integrate resources connected by shared institutional arrangements and the creation of mutual value through the exchange of services."[14]

Also, as "collaboration agreements through which companies combine their individual offerings into a coherent customer-oriented solution."[15]

The service ecosystem in its bimodal nature (face-to-face/virtual) is made up of the set of integrated services into the three pillars described above in what is called the service scope: personal or voluntary, public or collaborative, and private or exchange. Its structure is particularly distinguished by its bimodality, the autonomy of the entities, the services, and the engineering and architecture that integrate it.

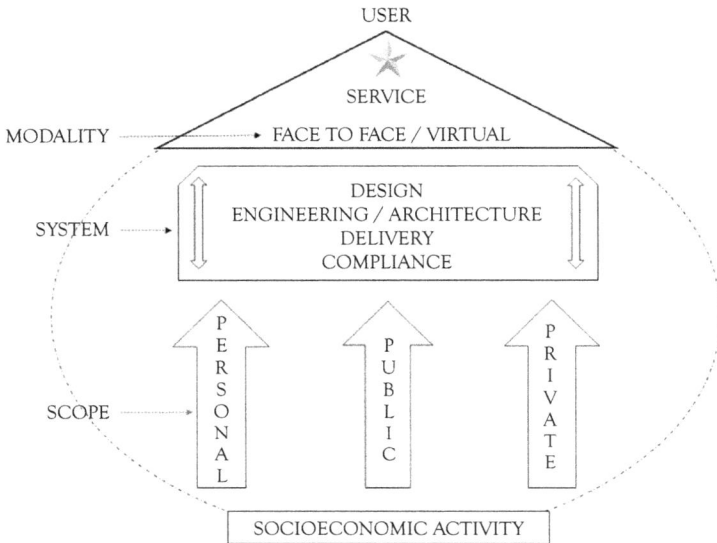

Figure 1.1 The service ecosystem

Taxonomy of Services

The user perception impacts on the service conception. This ability of the individual to interpret his or her environment through the stimuli that he or she captures through the sensory organs influences the creation and design of the service proposal. In this context, its validity, distinctive character, and value ensure its usefulness and acceptance, and require its conceptual consideration.

From the scope of servitization, the service can be considered from three typological perspectives: One, from the role of the service in society as the manifestations previously expressed as pillars of the service in personal, public, and private. A second internal and proprietary one referred to the very concept of service and developed in Roger Schmenner's "Service Process Matrix,"[16] which focuses on the degree of intensity of effort and the degree of interaction and personalization. And a third figure of general acceptance is related to economic activity, represented by

International Standard Industrial Classification of all economic activities (ISIC), Rev. 4,[17] and the international classification of products and services used for the registration of trademarks and patents (The Nice Classification (NCL)).[18]

It is to be observed from the general classification of economic activity by sectors in the 19th century that the service activity or tertiary sector has been approached from many perspectives without even integrating, due to the heterogeneity of activities and ambiguity of the concept, a theory general capable of defining a taxonomy of services.

On this occasion and from its economic perspective, the service ecosystem takes shape and reference from the "systematic classification of all economic activities whose purpose is to establish their harmonized coding at the global level (ISIC), considering that each country has, in generally, an industrial classification of its own, in the most appropriate way to respond to its individual circumstances and the degree of development of its economy."[19]

In this context, the Nice Classification established by the Nice Agreement (1957) for the registration of trademarks and patents serves with the ISIC as a valid reference to the subject and purpose of this work.

International Standard Industrial Classification of All Economic Activities (ISIC)

It is a classification of all economic activities by production processes that classify statistical units based on their main economic activity. Its purpose is to provide a set of activity categories that can be used for the collection, analysis, and presentation of statistics according to those activities and for the purposes of economic analysis, decision-making, and policy development. The categories in this classification are usually appropriate to each country as they vary from country to country and from region to region.

The following table illustrates the general structure of the economic activities of products and services contained in the ISIC 21 sections. The section of manufacturing is highlighted in bold by its particular attention in this work.

Table 1.1 General structure of the classification of economic activities

Section	Divisions	Description
A	01–03	Agriculture, forestry, and fishing
B	05–09	Mining and quarrying
C	10–33	**Manufacturing**
D	35	Electricity, gas, steam, and air-conditioning supply
E	36–39	Water supply; sewerage, waste management, and remediation activities
F	41–43	Construction
G	45–47	Wholesale and retail trade; repair of motor vehicles and motorcycles
H	49–53	Transportation and storage
I	55–56	Accommodation and food service activities
J	58–63	Information and communication
K	64–66	Financial and insurance activities
L	68	Real estate activities
M	69–75	Professional, scientific, and technical activities
N	77–82	Administrative and support service activities
O	84	Public administration and defense; compulsory social security
P	85	Education
Q	86–88	Human health and social work activities
R	90–93	Arts, entertainment and recreation
S	94–96	Other service activities
T	97–98	Activities of households as employers; undifferentiated goods- and services-producing activities of households for own use
U	99	Activities of extraterritorial organizations and bodies

Source: UN. 2009. International Standard Industrial Classification of All Economic Activities (ISIC), Rev.4, Statistical Papers (Ser. M), New York, NY: UN.

This classification also offers a detailed structure of these categories with two aggregations that make up *a decision tree* that serves not only its purpose of data collection, analysis, and presentation of statistics but also for commercial registration or certification to accredit its quality or comply with their tax and labor duties.

Likewise, it is a valid reference in the servitization process for the identification and location of a business opportunity in its specific economic sector, while contributing to the appropriate analysis in its context of innovation and sustainability.

Table 1.2 shows the section "C" of manufacturing industries of the detailed structure of the ISIC classification with an example of relevance and timeliness, the health industry.

The Healthcare Industry

Fortuitous or not, the coronavirus pandemic (COVID-19) phenomenon broke into the bowels of society, assaulted its welfare state, and disrupted the way of life, forcing it to protect and reconfigure it. This tragedy is promoting a new order of things and in the subject that concerns us, the productive activities of companies and businesses with greater severity to the health industries.

In this context, the pharmaceutical industry serves as a model to illustrate the process of locating and identifying service opportunities in a productive activity of an entity in the economic sector, using, as indicated before, the detailed ISIC scheme and its theoretical conception of *vertical/ horizontal integration* or multiple activities.

Section C: Manufacturing Industries (Sector)

It covers the physical or chemical transformation of materials, substances, or components into new products. The transformed materials, substances, or components are raw materials from the primary sector (agriculture, livestock, forestry, fishing, and mining and quarrying), as well as products from other manufacturing activities.

An economic entity, according to the ISIC concept, can be made up of one or several activities; then it must be classified according to the highest proportion of value added by the units that compose it, following the *descending method*.

The top-down method follows a hierarchical principle. The classification of a unit at the most detailed level of the classification must be consistent with its classification at the most aggregated levels.

Table 1.2 Classification of economic activities of the pharmaceutical industry according to ISIC

Division	Group	Class	Description
21			Manufacture of pharmaceuticals, medicinal chemicals, and botanicals products. This division includes the manufacture of basic pharmaceutical products and pharmaceutical preparations. The manufacture of medicinal chemicals and botanicals is also included.
	210		Manufacture of pharmaceuticals, medicinal chemicals, and botanicals for pharmaceutical

		2100	**This class includes:**
			• Manufacture of active medicinal substances that are used for their pharmacological properties in the manufacture of medicines: antibiotics, basic vitamins, salicylic, O-acetylsalicylic acids, etc.
			• Processing of blood
			  • Manufacture of medicaments
			  • Antisera and other blood fractions
			  • Vaccines
			• Diverse medicaments, including homeopathic preparations
			• Manufacture of chemical contraceptive products for external use and hormonal contraceptive medicaments
			• Manufacture of preparations for medical diagnosis preparations, including pregnancy tests
			• Manufacture of radioactive in-vivo diagnostic substances
			• Manufacture of biotech pharmaceuticals
			This class also includes:
			• Manufacture of chemically pure sugars
			• Processing of glands and manufacture of extracts of glands, etc.
			• Manufacture of medical impregnated wadding, gauze, bandages, dressings, etc.
			• Preparation of botanical products (grinding, grading, milling) for pharmaceutical use
			This class excludes:
			• Manufacture of herbal infusions (mint, vervain, chamomile, etc.); see 1079
			• Manufacture of dental fillings and dental cements, see class 3250
			• Manufacture of bone reconstruction cements, see class 3250
			• Wholesale of pharmaceutical, see class 4649
			• Retail sale of pharmaceutical, see class 4772
			• Research and development for pharmaceutical and biotech pharmaceutical, see class 7210
			• Packaging of Pharmaceutical, see class 8292

Source: UN. 2009. International Standard Industrial Classification of All Economic Activities (ISIC), Rev.4, Statistical Papers (Ser. M), New York, NY: UN.

Vertical integration (vertical and horizontal in the concept of this work) occurs when the same activity gives rise to end products with different characteristics. It can be understood that these are activities carried out simultaneously using the same factors of production, although it might be unlikely to separate these activities into different processes, assign them to different units, or generally provide separate data on them. In this case, the criteria based on the imputation of added value or similar methods could not be applied to them. In this regard, there is no uniformly valid criterion to identify the activity that best represents the set that encompasses this horizontal integration; so the best criterion of auxiliary, mixed, multiple, independent, derived, or related activities is commonly adopted and referred to them and integrates into classes considered related or that may seem similar, to another division or section, observed in the table.

The Nice Classification (NCL)

It is an international classification of products and services that applies specifically to the registration of trademarks and patents. It is mandatory not only for registering trademarks at the national level in the States party to the Nice Agreement but also for the international registration of trademarks.

"It is a classification, consisting of an alphabetical list of **34 classes of goods**, adopted under the Nice Agreement and subsequently expanded to cover **11 classes of services** and the corresponding alphabetical list of those services."[20]

The following table in accordance with the ISIC classification shows class 5 corresponding to *pharmaceutical products* contained in the Nice Classification and for the purposes of this work, which offer a vision of the possibilities of productive activities from another perspective.

These typologies show the magnitude of the spectrum of *pure products* (manufacturing) and services associated with products that make up the service ecosystem. At the same time, they articulate the different phases of the chain of production and services activities, and of analytical tools to identify possible and feasible opportunities to add value to the current main business model or by resorting to activities in related alternative chains.

Table 1.3 Classification of pharmaceutical products (class 5) according to the Nice Classification

Class	Products (Description)
5	Pharmaceuticals, medical and veterinary preparations; sanitary preparations for medical purposes; dietetic food and substances adapted for medical or veterinary use, food for babies; dietary supplements for human beings and animals; plasters, materials for dressings; material for stopping teeth, dental wax; disinfectants; preparations for destroying vermin; fungicides, herbicides. **This Class includes, in particular:** • sanitary preparations for personal hygiene, other than toiletries • diapers for babies and for incontinence • deodorants, other than for human beings or for animals • medicated shampoos, soaps, lotions, and dentifrices • dietary supplements intended to supplement a normal diet or to have health benefits • meal replacements and dietetic food and beverages adapted for medical or veterinary use **This Class does not include, in particular:** • ingredients for use in the manufacture of pharmaceuticals, for example, vitamins, preservatives, and antioxidants (Cl. 1) • sanitary preparations being nonmedicated toiletries (Cl. 3) • deodorants for human beings or for animals (Cl. 3) • support bandages and orthopedic bandages (Cl. 10) • meal replacements and dietetic food and beverages not specified as being for medical or veterinary use, which should be classified in the appropriate food or beverage classes, for example, low-fat potato crisps (Cl. 29), high-protein cereal bars (Cl. 30), and isotonic beverages (Cl. 32).

Source: The Nice Classification / www.wipo.int/classifications/nice/en

The Service Business Model

A service business model is a theoretical scheme that clearly defines what value proposition is offered to a market, which user it is aimed at, how it is implemented, how it is delivered, how it corresponds to the proposal, how it is measured, and how profit is.

This structure has been studied from the manufacturing organizations to know the properties of the service activities and how they are distinguished from the traditional manufacturing ones. As a result of this search, two well-known systematic conceptual schemes emerge: the *service profit chain*, inserted in the *strategic service vision*.[21]

(a) **The service value chain** postulates that the profit and growth of any organization or business result from customer loyalty, generated by customer satisfaction, which is a function of the value delivered to the customer.

Similarly, customer value is the result of employee loyalty and productivity, a function of employee satisfaction, directly related to internal quality or value created by employees. Today, the widespread use by the management of this service pathway as a proven via of success in delivering the expected results to users allows it to consider as a driver of profitability and company growth.

(b) **The strategic vision of the service** is a systematic way of thinking about the service strategy of a business to carry out the components of the service value chain. In the context of a servitization strategy, the aforementioned scheme would serve as a reference to a five-phase format that fits the proposal of this work, and it is detailed below: 1) users and places, 2) the service proposal, 3) the operational strategy, 4) the delivery system, and 5) the compliance management. This corresponds to the theoretical scheme of the business model and serves as guidance for its application to organizations or service businesses activities.

1. **Users and places**. To whom and where the service proposal addressed. To precise the places and possible users with potential willingness to acquire the service, some questions are suggested:

    - **User profile.** Qualities that identify and distinguish the users.

    - **Scope.** The differentiated homogeneous groups to which the service proposal is directed.

    - **Need and expectation.** Gaps, solutions, and expectations that the service proposal undertakes to fulfill.

    - **Share.** The competition, company(s), or institution (s) that offer(s) a similar or analogous service in the market.

    - **Capability**. The operational capability used to compete and serve the needs, solutions, and expectations of the user.

    - **Excellence.** The level of quality of the service offered satisfies or resolves the user's shortcomings, expectations, concerns, or difficulties.

2. **The service proposal.** The document that describes in detail the concept, qualities, and differentiating elements that make up the

service to be provided. This is the fundamental information for the service design. Likewise, and together with the information of the *target market*, they establish the *differentiating element* of the service and define its *positioning* in the market. This is the image that the brand of a service or product occupies in the mind of the user. Positioning that it is built from the perception formed by the user of the service individually and with respect to the competition.

In section "C" on the service, systematicity, and transversality, described earlier in this chapter, you will find the answers to the following questions about this basic and integrating element of the strategic vision of a service:

- **Constituent.** All the components, properties, or qualities that give a specific and differentiating shape to the service and the value proposition.
- **User perception.** The perception that the user has of each attribute of the service.
- **Service perception.** The perception, image, or idea that the service projects on the user or market: quality and value for the customer.
- **Work and resources.** The necessary capabilities and resources to successfully carry out the service proposal.

3. **The operational strategy.** The process of management and successful achievement of the action of providing or supplying the service.

- **Factors**. Key operating factors that guarantee service compliance.
- **Points of attention.** The key point(s) of operation(s) and/or contact(s) where greater attention and vigor are required in the correct and satisfactory fulfillment of the service.
- **Resources placement.** Determination of the element, situation, or phase of the process where the placement of resources of any kind is required.
- **Efficiency.** Determine in the process what is going to be controlled, establish measurement units, set measurement

standards, procedures and processes, and establish preventive and corrective actions.

- **Positioning.** Establish the conditions, behavior, and expected achievements to meet the objectives and outperform the competition.

4. **The delivery system.** The set of interrelated activities that make it possible for the user to get the requested service on time, in the right place and with satisfaction. The delivery system is an integrated element that is established in support of the strategy and its identity is configured by answering the following questions:

- **Key points.** Identifies the point of contact or interaction with the greatest attention, interest, or performance in the service provision process based on the attributes (time, cost, etc.) specified in the proposal to the user.
- **Capacity.** The space, skills, and necessary resources to provide the service.
- **Excellence assurance.** The delivery, fulfillment, and measurement of the service in correspondence with the value proposition and the user needs and expectations.
- **Differentiation.** The attribute(s) that make the service a unique proposition in the market.
- **Entry barriers.** Identification of the factors that place limits or difficulties on the entry of new similar service proposals: investment, differentiation, communication, technological innovation, and so on.

5. **The compliance management.** The faithful fulfillment assurance of the value promise is a key indicator of success in a service business model. This phase closes the process cycle and is developed later in the third part of this publication.

The Activity/Performance as a Service Model (APAAS)

To the principles and approaches of the service business model, described so far and considered essentially based on its face-to-face modality, it should be added as an information in the context of the service ecosystem.

The virtual service business models, conceived as abstractions of the information technology services of a company, are aimed at developing solutions as services and used as applications for their design.

In addition to the management models of information technology services such as ITIL for its acronym in English, models or tools are available for the implementation of structured services in the cloud and that operate as they would in a physical structure. Some of these, they are known as *Infrastructure* as a service (IaaS), *Platform* as a service (PaaS), and *Software* as a service (SaaS).

Application Exercise

Purpose

The following exercise seeks to integrate in a practical way the knowledge, methods, and tools indicated in this chapter on the service value chain. It also attempts to strengthen the possible learning and its subsequent use in academic, business, and entrepreneurial contexts.

Identify, analyze, and design a service business opportunity of your interest or select a productive activity from the categories (23) of **manufacturing industries** contained in the International Standard Industrial Classification of all economic activities (ISIC) of the United Nations.

Apply the content developed in the aforementioned chapter, noting:
- The ecosystem of the corresponding service
- The fundamentals of the applied service
- The business model with the components of the service design

Outcome

Design project of a service value proposition.

Final Acknowledgment

By completing this application exercise, the reader will have appropriated the knowledge developed in Chapter 1 and acquired effective skills for putting it into practice in real business contexts.

CHAPTER 2

Servitization

An Assessment Holistic Perspective

When companies seek to activate, achieve, improve their results and benefits, strengthen their competitiveness, and encourage sustainable growth as a business, a first obligatory look is to its interior and to the analysis of its proposal and strategy of co-creation of value with its consumer/user. This contingency, always present and changing of a business in an increasingly dynamic and competitive market, also guides, on occasions of despair and inspiration, to the search and external analysis of opportunities, proposals, or additions, related or alien to the very essence of business.

This internal or external search by the company is not exclusive to any sector of economic activity but the result of the resilient capability of companies over time. In this context, industries have chosen to rethink their *raison d'être* and pay particular attention to their social fabric to investigate their value-creation process, the link with the end user or business customer.

Since the 1960s, the literature has registered with greater precision and importance the client's issue as the reason for the existence of a business as well as the attention to service as an encounter and interaction in the search for solutions and satisfaction of needs and priorities.

The framework of an industry's organizational values resumed, renewed, and placed its focus on the principles of *Customer orientation* and *Service vocation* as the foundations of its strategic orientation with its employees to fulfill the commitment to achieve customer satisfaction with *quality* standards.

The approach and management of the business service continued to be consolidated with the service culture through the development of a mentality and own service style (differentiation), expanding the concept of service to *Shared services*[1] as a strategy for efficiency, competitiveness, and value addition to the own business units, extending to *advanced services* (ADS)[2] as activities (diversification) intended for sale as *intermediate consumption*, goods, or merchandise that exhaust their production process and that may or may not be acquired by other economic entities, until the appearance in 1988 of the construct "Servitization"[3] to signify the movement of the manufacturing industry toward the addition of services to add value to the business.

Today, this orientation has evolved with the contribution of the emerging Service Science to more advanced concepts, applications, and experiences to attend to the current complex business environment, managing to become an imminent and urgent matter. Thus, we have service system as a business and innovation model,[4, 5, 6] or product-service system,[7, 8, 9] as a service aggregation depending on the perspective research on the topic: servitization or product-service system.

The service inherence and transversality qualities in all socio-economic activities, the evolution of service knowledge, and the results of servitization experiences in manufacturing companies serve the purpose of this work. It offers the business contingency of adding value to the business, a holistic perspective of the service as a resilient and dynamic capability to the process of adoption and implementation of a servitization strategy.

How to identify, assess, adopt, and implement a servitization initiative? The following diagram shows the assessment process detailed below:

Table 2.1 Assessment process

1. **The motivation of adoption**
   a. You don't always start with finances
   b. Organizational values and personal beliefs
2. **The assessment perspective**
   A. The business integral value chain
   B. Servitization
   C. The comprehensive assessment tree
      a. Principles and assessment criteria
      b. Top-down method
      c. Assessment categories
3. **Service business opportunity**
   A. Service option
   B. Business opportunity
   C. Decision to adopt and add the service
   D. Application process

The Motivation of Adoption

You Don't Always Start With Finances

The situational factor and willingness to adopt a servitization strategy are for the company management, first, a personal managerial challenge of a cultural nature and a matter of conceptual elucidation in the face of a business challenge.

Beyond myths, misinterpretations, and its polysemic character, the word *service* still recalls the idea of servitude and is commonly associated with semi-skilled jobs or low-paid jobs in economic activity and is identified as those performed by hotel and restaurant employees, banks, among others.

However, the prominence of the service in contemporary society, in economic activity and the evidence of advances in knowledge on the subject along with the high participation in the workforce of highly qualified professional and business service categories such as health, education, finances, TICs, and so on, indicates that the services cannot be estimated or labeled as something of low value.

Organizational Values and Personal Beliefs

The acceptance, commitment, and fulfillment of the service are other factors of attention of the company's direction and management,[10] relevant to the success of a servitization proposal. The studies carried out so far show little or moderate attention to the *principle of acceptance* of the service as the company is more focused on other areas such as products, technology, and the consumer.

Acceptance of business service involves a cultural environment formed by the system of beliefs and personal values that shape the attitude and behavior of individuals in the organization: an assessment of its usefulness, a service mindset, an assumed commitment, an effort of make and publicize what is proposed, a delivery of what was promised, and the achievement of compliance to the satisfaction of the participants of the interaction.

Compliance with this *principle* will make the organization feel more comfortable, will provide greater purpose and commitment, and will strengthen compliance efforts with the user/costumer, ensuring satisfaction as a key indicator of service success and business opportunity.

The company leadership in the face of any situational contingency factor will consider the relevance and specific value that the possible option considered has for the company. In the case of the adoption of a servitization strategy, the alignment of organizational values with the beliefs and personal values of the direction and management of the company significantly influences not only the valuation process but also constitutes a committed challenge for the company acceptance, implementation, and success in the service business opportunity.

What value does the service bring to one's business?

1. The service is inherent to the human being and a conscious value for the user who demands it and is willing to compensate for its quality level.
2. In its character as a social entity, the organization is also consubstantial to the service that is present in the process of creative interaction of company value with its user/consumer.
3. Advances in the service knowledge of unprecedented and with a sustained expansionary trend and the development of information and communication technologies have managed to change not only the traditional way of meeting needs and the creation of new ones but to transform our way of living and working.

   This evolution of services has reached preeminent value in the world economic activity and labor force, as well as a disruption in the conception, management, and direction of businesses and organizations, both public and private.
4. The high-quality service (excellence) confers distinctive character, prestige, and gives brand value to the company. This is essential in the marketing and consumer/user/customer engagement process.
5. The perspective of the service-dominant logic as an alternative to the traditional product-dominant logic in the economic exchange as a process of value co-creation[11] makes a convenient contribution to businesses in their purposes of innovation and sustainability in highly challenging markets.

What is the managerial attitude of a service environment?

This is an organizational challenge that has its response in the company dynamic capability to develop in its personnel the necessary soft skills to make change management possible and take advantage of the opportunities offered by the service ecosystem. Later in Chapter 4 of this work, this organizational capability is discussed in detail.

The Assessment Perspective

The servitization construct has been sustained through its widespread application and implementation in the manufacturing industry since its emergence in 1988.[12] The concept is associated with challenges and risks, considering that the change in the model from manufacturing (product) to service (solutions) goes beyond adding services to the product offering.

In this context, the concept is here expanded to be applied without distinction in all sectors of economic activity as an instrument for viewing, approaching, and validating business opportunities in the service ecosystem, to respond to business contingency.

What key preconditions should the company management address to assess, assume, and overcome the challenges of the decision to adopt a servitization process?

In this second phase of the servitization process, two concurrent factors are considered: the business integral value chain and the assessment matrix of a business idea.

The Business Integral Value Chain

It serves the concept of value creation[13] as an instrument for analyzing business activity through which it is separated into its constituent parts to identify opportunities that generate value.

From this perspective, the value chain approach[14, 15] as an integrating axis and analysis factor bases the adoption process, considering that the conception or acceptance of a servitization strategy implies for the management of the manufacturing company. Beyond one's own motivations and the mere addition of services to the product offering, a management must understand the challenge of the differences and impact between the activities of the current business, the convenience of developing shared services, and the possible opportunities that may offer the incorporation of associated or related services.

The theory of vertical integration,[16] commonly observed in a business when it is dedicated to the different aspects of production from raw materials, manufacturing, storage, transportation, distribution, and sale to the final consumer, that is, end-to-end integration all the way through the product's life cycle, gives rise to what is now known as the company's integral value chain.

A classic example of vertical integration is in the oil industry, which brings together under its control activities as diverse as exploration, drilling, production, transportation, refining, storage, packaging, distribution, marketing, and retail of the products it manufactures. In this context, there is vertical integration of activities when the different production phases are carried out successively in the same unit and when the product of one process serves as an input for the next.

In the case of horizontal or lateral integration theory, it occurs when a company acquires, merges, or creates another or other companies that carry out the same activity, produce goods of the same type or that can be substitutes, and it is done with the purpose of achieving cover other market segments, increase their participation, and power within it. Unlike vertical integration, its purposes are complementary.

Distinctive and well-known examples of horizontal integration are the acquisitions of Exxon-Mobil, Coca-Cola-Jugos del Valle, and Mattel-Fisher Price, among other manufacturing companies.

In the servitization strategy context, the horizontal integration process is also referred to the identification and analysis of services associated with the goods or products of the productive activity that may be capable of adding value to the manufacturing business.

This conception of ownership and control style of a company offers two varieties of integration, vertical and horizontal, which are combined to generate an *integral model* frequently used in manufacturing companies and made up of the multiple and diverse chain of a business activities.

The ISIC format, previously described in the service taxonomy section, serves to the servitization process as an integrating axis, support and search tool and location analysis and identification of opportunities for adding value to the company. This structure disaggregates economic activity to the most detailed levels of productive activities of industries and groups of industries, as well as to the most aggregated levels of economic sectors. Likewise, it allows observing and examining the economic interactions between the different activities and understanding the links of the productive scaffolding of the economy.

Servitization

The concepts of servitization and integral model (theory of vertical and horizontal integration) mentioned above are closely related,[17] particularly if one observes the process of servicing that has been progressively incorporated into the activity of companies since the initial *customer orientation* and a *vocation of service* until today known as *advanced services* (ADS) and the *intelligent service* (smart service) due to their relationship with manufactured products and technological advances.

This is how this assessment perspective serves in this proposal as an integrating axis of the organizational service ecosystem, while expanding the scope of the servitization concept. It is a holistic vision of the business service ecosystem that unfolds from its strategic cultural development in organizational performance (service culture). It adds value to the constituent units of the business (shared services), the identification and addition of value through business service opportunities (servitization), and intermediary activities (advanced services) in the company's value chain. This process of the company servitizicing is presented in its implementation levels in the following table:

Table 2.2 The evolution of service in the manufacturing company

Level	Concept	Description
1	Service business	*Organizational change: customer orientation/service vocation/service culture*
2	Shared services	*Adding value to the company business units*
3	Servitization	*Addition of services to the value chain of the manufacturing business*
4	Advanced services	*Intermediary service activities*
5	Smart service	*Digital data management service collected and analyzed based on smart grids, platforms, and technical systems*

This conjunction of conceptual parameters, integral business value chain, service profit chain,[18] the emerging theory of service science,[19] the here expanded concept of servitization[20] in relation to the integrated model (Theory of vertical/ horizontal integration), makes possible the following structure of analysis, assessment, and support of the servitization initiatives of companies and businesses.

The Comprehensive Assessment Tree

It is the integration axis and disaggregation of a defined productive activity. It organizes the detailed information of the constituent parts of the activity being evaluated, following a vertical and horizontal arrangement, and in accordance with some principles, criteria, and categories for the purpose of decision-making.

Principles and Assessment Criteria

The assessment structure is based on two principles:

(a) The *sector or productive activity*, not in the establishment or company. A company is an institutional entity that produces goods and services. An economic agent with autonomy to make financial and investment decisions, with authority to allocate resources and carry out one or more productive activities.

(b) The valuation is established from the *categories of productive activity* of the economic entity.

The relevant endpoints are:

(a) *The opportunities for added service* generated from the categories of the productive activity of the establishment or company.

(b) *The additional economic value* generated by the services added to the production process.

(c) *The end user* as the central purpose of the value proposition of the added services.

Top-Down Method

The process of determining a business category of activities follows a hierarchical principle that is descending and consistent with the activity in relation to its more detailed level of aggregates to progressively less aggregated levels. The top-down method is applied as follows:

Case: Pharmaceutical Activity

Step 1: Determine **the sector of economic activity** that corresponds to the business.

Sector: Manufacturing activities

Step 2: Determine **the productive activity** to which the establishment or company is engaged and to which the largest proportion of the added value corresponds.

Productive activity (higher added value):

Manufacture of pharmaceutical products, medicinal chemicals, and botanical products for pharmaceutical use.

Step 3: Determine **the main economic activity** of the business; the one that contributes the greatest proportion of the added value to the entity.

Main economic activity

Manufacture of medicines:

• Antisera and other blood fractions

• Vaccines

• Various medicines, including homeopathic preparations

Step 4: Within the main economic activity of the business, determine the **secondary economic activity**, independent activity that generates products through third or secondary parties.

Secondary economic activity:

Manufacture of herbal teas (mint, verbena, chamomile, etc.); retail of pharmaceutical products; or research and development for pharmaceutical products that may be part of another sector of activities such as the manufacture of food products.

Step 5: Within the productive activity of the business, primary and secondary, determine **the auxiliary activities**, those that support the productive activity of the entity and generate perishable products or services for the main or exclusive use of the company.

Auxiliary activity:

Logistics services, general services, business processes, telemarketing, and so on.

Step 6: Determine **the horizontally integrated activities**. This category of activity is transversal and is identified when the same activity (primary or secondary) gives rise to final products or services with different characteristics.

Horizontal activity:

The manufacture of various drugs according to their active principle: prevention, diagnosis, or treatment of a disease or pathological state, or to modify physiological systems for the benefit of the person to whom it is administered.

Assessment Categories

The valuation categories are established through the subdivision of the productive activity in a hierarchical structure vertically and horizontally integrated by six levels of mutually exclusive categories identified as 1) sector of economic activity, 2) productive activity of the business, 3) main activity, 4) secondary activity, 5) auxiliary activity, and 6) horizontally integrated activity. These unbundling action activities make it possible to locate and identify service options within a broad horizon of the servitization process.

Next, each of the category levels is detailed, and by way of illustration, how the process of determining service opportunities is carried out, using the productive activity of manufacturing as a model, pharmaceutical industry, and following a falling procedure:

Sector of Economic Activity

It is the first level or valuation phase. Economic activity is traditionally divided into three economic sectors, attending to the production process and integrating a chain of activities aimed at obtaining products and services: primary or agricultural sector, secondary or manufacturing sector, and tertiary sector or service sector.

Recently, there has been talk of a new sector: the quaternary. This is considered as a division of the tertiary sector based on intellectual or knowledge activities such as consulting, research, strategic planning, and so on.

These integrated economic activities, with common characteristics and differentiating elements in relation to other groups, offer a panoramic view of the economic sector and constitute the first phase of orientation and analysis in the search for opportunities.

- In which sector of economic activity is the business located?
- What is the significance and magnitude of its contribution to the economic sector?
- What is your level of competitiveness?

Case: Pharmaceutical Industry.   Business sector dedicated to the manufacture, preparation, and commercialization of medicinal chemical products for the treatment and the prevention of diseases.

Sector of economic activity: Manufacturing activities

Activities mainly dedicated to the physical or chemical transformation of materials, substances, or components into new products. These manufacturing activities are known as factories or plants and are characterized by the use of machinery and equipment to handle materials and substances.

Productive Business Activity

The integral chain (vertical and horizontal) of the business productive activities or the economic entity, from its origin, occurs when the different production phases are carried out successively in the same unit and when the product of one process serves as an input for the next. It serves as a valid reference for the second phase of location and identification of possible service opportunities: the main productive activity.

The productive activity is the transformation of inputs (raw materials, human, material, or financial resources, etc.), whose results, goods, products, or services can be transferred, traded, or used in the satisfaction of needs, as required solutions or for their own benefit.

The business productive activity is the spectrum of vertically integrated activities that constitute the company, carry out activities with specific purposes, and generate benefits or provide value proportionally in the development cycle of a product or service.

This phase facilitates the identification and separation of the constituent parts of the current business and offers a flow of information, essential for its subsequent analysis and evaluation.

- What productive activity is the business engaged in?
- What is the integral value chain (end-to-end) of the business?

Case: Pharmaceutical Industry

Productive Business Activity
Manufacture of pharmaceutical products, medicinal chemicals, and botanical products for pharmaceutical use.

Service Opportunity
Pharmaceutical entities or drug companies can produce the materials or contract with other units to produce those materials for them.

Main Economic Activity

The activity to which the company is engaged and whose resulting product or by-product adds greater value to the economic entity.

- What is the main activity and result of the business?
- Does the productive activity contain other activity(s) that may be considered for addition to the business?

Case: Pharmaceutical Industry

Main Economic Activity
A pharmaceutical entity may comprise as its main economic activity one or more of the following activities:

- Manufacture of active medicinal substances that are used for their pharmacological properties in the manufacture

of medicines: antibiotics, basic vitamins, salicylic acid, acetylsalicylic acid, and so on.
- Manufacture of medicines:
  ○ Antisera and other blood fractions
  ○ Vaccines
  ○ Various medicines, including homeopathic preparations

Service Opportunity
Pharmaceutical entities or pharmaceutical companies can prepare substances or medicines as well as contract other units or entities to elaborate those materials or medicines in their place.

Note:
The reference model details all the activities known and possible as the main activity in an economic entity; noting, however, that the limits of these activities in the sector or entity (pharmaceutical) may be imprecise. This is shown with the aggregations that are made in the opportunity of the periodic reviews as well as the inclusion of new additions, particularly services, made by the entities in an independent or pertinent sectorial manner.

Secondary Economic Activity

Any independent activity that, through a transformation process, generates products or results with added value, ultimately destined for third parties. Most economic entities produce some secondary product.

- What is (are) the activity(s) and secondary result(s) of the business?
- What aggregations would be possible?

Case: Pharmaceutical Industry. A pharmaceutical entity can generate products or results for third parties:

- Retail sale of pharmaceutical products (drugstores or pharmacies)
- Research and development for pharmaceutical products (e.g., covid-19 vaccine)

- Packaging of pharmaceutical products (e.g., containers for laboratory analysis samples)

Service Opportunity

In the case of pharmaceutical entities or pharmaceutical companies, their market scope is wide and in the context of the sector productive activity or of the business economic activity, the possibility of adding services is also extensive, as shown the sustained growth of the service sector and in particular the health sector.

Auxiliary Activity

The main and secondary activities cannot be carried out without the support of various ancillary activities. These serve to support or make possible the execution or achievement of the main production activity of an economic entity, generating nondurable products or services for the main or exclusive use of said entity.

Auxiliary activities in any business can be identified in company accounting, storage, transportation, purchases, sales promotion, cleaning, repairs, maintenance, and security, among others.

Ancillary activities exist to support the primary production activities of an entity by generating nondurable products or services for the primary or exclusive use of that entity.

What is (are) the auxiliary activity(s) and result(s) of the business?

Case: Pharmaceutical Industry

Service Opportunity

- Who carries out these activities in or for the company?
- Which one (s) would be (are) directly related to the end user/ consumer?
- What shared value (user/business) could it add?

Horizontally Integrated Activity

This category of activity is transversal, and it is the productive activity of an economic entity when it gives rise to final products with different characteristics and made simultaneously, using the same production factors.

These activities whose economic effects are complex to separate or assign them to different units, the criteria based on the imputation of added value or similar methods could not be applied to them; however, they constitute areas susceptible to inquiry in the search for opportunities.

Case: Pharmaceutical Industry

Service Opportunity
Some activities of this category in the pharmaceutical industry could be part of manufacturing industries for the production of food products, such as "Manufacture of herbal teas (mint, verbena, chamomile, and so on,"[21] among others.

Service Business Opportunity

Service Option

The main source of service option(s) as detailed in the previous phase of the comprehensive valuation tree is in the company comprehensive value. Through scrutiny of the end-to-end and transversal process, starting from the location of the economic entity with its main productive activity, the possible service options are identified. To the extent that the main productive activity occupies a strategic position in the economic sector, the greater the possibility of service opportunity.

There is the possibility of other collateral sources of ideas or service opportunities, related or independent, that merit their study separately.

In the context of the servitization process, the service option is recognized according to the principle of *orientation to the end user*, assuming the relevance of the service for the company and its purpose. The four-factor analysis contributes to its resolution and possible adoption:

1. **Productive activity:** Economic attractiveness and location of the company in the integral value chain
2. **Target market:** Size, location, purchasing power, and viability

3. **Economic feasibility:** The cost-benefit, commercial attractiveness, and business potential
4. **Collaterality:** Ability to integrate with activities from other sectors

Business Opportunity

Having identified the possible service option(s) from the company productive activity, the business opportunity foundation follows. This is defined with particular attention to two central perspectives: the end user and the market opportunity.

Where to focus attention?

End User

(a) Needs and expectations (tastes and preferences)
(b) Market inefficiencies (quality of service)
(c) Market players (competition)
(d) Market size and purchasing power (sufficiency)

Market Opportunity

(a) The service proposal (attractiveness and added value)
(b) Required resources (availability)
(c) Financial feasibility (indicators)
  • Net present value (NPV)
  • Internal rate of return (IRR)
  • EBITDA (earnings before interest taxes depreciation and amortization)

Decision to Adopt and Add the Service

The decision to add value to the business by adding service is the closing of a reasoned and consensual management process that responds to the service business opportunity and ensures the adequate implementation of its strategy and the achievement of the proposed results.

At this level of the integral analysis process (vertical and horizontal), it is assumed that the company has decided to adopt the servitization strategy to add service to the business that allows it to connect directly with the end user.

The next action corresponds to the service business opportunity implementation process. The various project management tools and applications are good allies to carry out this purpose.

Application Process

The Fuel Expenditure (Gas Station/Service Station). The oil industry is a classic example of *vertical integration* (end-to-end). A company that integrates under its control and ownership and different productive activities such as 1) exploration, 2) production, 3) transportation, 4) refining, 5) storage, 6) distribution, 7) marketing, and 8) retail (*sale of liquid fuels derived from petroleum*) from the products of its transformation process.

The fuel expenditure (service/gas station) is the most visible image of the oil industry in the market and the last link in its integral value chain. It is your direct contact with the end user: the vehicle driver.

This establishment operates as a business unit of the oil industry that can be managed by the owning oil company or given in concession to an individual or another company, generally private.

1. A gas station is a service establishment directly related to the sector of economic activity: extraction of crude oil.
2. The productive activity that corresponds to its business: manufacture of products derived from hydrocarbons.
3. The *main economic activity* of a gas station is *the sale of fuels, lubricants and/or vehicular natural gas* (NGV), and/or *compressed natural gas* (CNG) that contributes the largest proportion of the value added to the establishment. The NGV and CNG are integrated. It may or may not be part of the sale. The market determines it. In the oil industry, gas has its own integral value chain. Conceptually here, it is considered *a horizontal activity*.

4. A gas station also performs secondary economic activity by providing automotive lubricant change services as well as washing, greasing, and lubrication services for automobiles. These activities are directly related to the productive activity of the industry (liquid and semi-solid lubricants) whose proportion of value added to the business is lower.

5. The fuels transportation and the establishment security are, among others, auxiliary activities of the gas station that, for own use and support of the activities of the establishment, are susceptible to additional services with added value contribution. These services can be contracted or assumed as business units of the outlet.

6. The *diversification* of a gas station is carried out from the main economic activity, by adding horizontal activities (related or independent): the convenience store, the tire repair service, the vending machines, and emerging travel centers, such as **Bu-cce's** in the state of Texas, (https://buc-ees.com), among other service business opportunities.

This process of application of the integral valuation tree for the identification of service business opportunities is based on the perspective of productive/economic activity, the theories of vertical integration, and the emerging Science of Service. It strengthens the concept of servitization, serves its operational purpose, and references a reliable scheme of innovation and business growth policies.

The theory of vertical integration has been applied with great success in numerous cases, not only in the manufacturing industry such as textile, automotive, pharmaceutical companies, and so on, but also in the field of agribusiness to agricultural products and derivatives, forestry, and other natural resources, when companies have taken over the activities related to their integral value chain.

Emblematic Examples of Servitization[22]

There are many examples in the economic activity and in the manufacturing industry that have significantly and successfully evolved their business models over time and under concepts, such as *diversification, integration, or concentration*, and now under servitization when conceiving or specifically adding services to its integral value chain. This is done through the use of the concepts, methods, and tools described in this work. Some of the more well-known cases are briefly described below:

Oil Industry

It is the classic example of manufacturing companies that bring together activities as diverse as exploration, drilling, production (extraction), transportation, refining (processing), warehousing, commercial distribution, and retail. In other words, its products are delivered under the modality of direct or delegated control to the end user/consumer.

The integral value chain of the business in this industry has been developed by applying the theory or strategy of "vertical integration" (vertical and horizontal) that breaks down economic activity by production processes as shown by the International Standard Industrial Classification (ISIC) of all economic activities, which has served as a reference to the treatment of the subject in this work.

The application scheme that takes as a reference to the gas/service station and is described in Chapter 2 illustrates the concept and process of servitization in this industrial sector.

Coca-Cola

Coca-Cola's system and its value chain. A centennial business (1886), based on the sale of soft drinks, considers itself as "a catalyst for social interaction and inspired innovation." It operates in a broad context from which it continually learns to manage its impacts and create shared opportunities "as we transform into a total beverage company."

> Our short- and long-term success depends on a variety of inputs, such as ingredients, water, and packaging from our many suppliers, and on the talent and passion of our global workforce and system employees. And, of course, our business generates income from consumers who give us their trust and the financial resources to operate, innovate, and grow.

In its effort to maintain its presence, growth, and influence in the soft drink and related markets globally, it constantly draws on its integral value chain to "create a variety of results that include diverse beverage products. These economic benefits include jobs, taxes paid, and community investment, ecosystem impacts and initiatives, and value for the customer and the shareholder."

With this perspective, it acquires (2007) *Jugos del Valle*, a juice company with the purpose of expanding its beverage portfolio mainly in Latin America; likewise, to "Powerade," an energy drink to cover other fronts of the market. It purchases manufacturing plants for packaging and packaging material and invests significant resources in a variety of services related to delivery, encounter points, and the consumer experiences with its products to ensure continuity of supply, quality, and variety, and in particular, maintain permanent contact with its end consumers.

Source: www.coca-cola.com/.

Apple

Who is Apple's main hardware and software vendor?

Who makes Apple devices?

How do Apple products reach the end user: iPhones, iPads, iWatches, and MacBooks?

Through its own stores, distributors, and authorized service providers. Among technology companies, Apple stands out for the proven quality of its products and services, proving to be a market agent that is difficult to imitate.

This company maintains under its command the control of tasks and activities that are key for its contact, contribution, and maintenance of a significantly different experience for the user, while strengthening its long-range competitive advantage.

Its comprehensive value chain is illustrated in Table 2.3.

The control strategy of the activities of its integral value chain extends from the creation and design of components for its processors (hardware), continuing with its programs (software) to direct distribution to the end user through its own stores (iShops) and authorized service providers (Apple Premium Reseller).

Source: www.apple.com/.

Table 2.3 Integral value chain

Product	Program	Service	Content
Chips/Accessories (AirPods)	OS X	iMessage	iTunes, iTunes Radios, Beats
iMac, MacBook, MacPro, Mac Mini	iOS	Face Time	iTunes
iPad	Safari	Maps	App Store
iPhone	iWork, iLife	iCloud	App Store
Apple Watch	Desktop and mobile apps	Mail	iBooks
Apple TV	iCloud, iTunes App Store	Apple Pay	Kiosk

Inditex

It is a business model, compensated or end-to-end integration, and a case study in the textile and fashion industry that, from its centralized structure, works with a concentrated network of nonexclusive factories around the world, and through code of conduct and agreements on all kinds of matters. They produce the designs that they send for marketing through a logistics system that is also their own to their direct sales network to the final consumer (Zara, Pull & Bear, Massimo Dutti, Bershka, Stradivarius, Oysho, etc.).

In this context, most of its brands with a high level of outsourcing renew their collections between four and six times a year, by responding quickly to market needs and controlling a large part of the supply chain. It achieves a high turnover of its products permanently creating a sense of urgency among customers; if they like a product, it is better to buy it rather than to avoid it, not to see it again for a long time.

Thus store employees and other specialists the brand has in leading fashion centers play a role of significant value. They have the mission of reporting to the company's headquarters in Spain, information on newness that customers are looking for, as well as on new styles and trends that fashion impose in cities like New York or Paris. As a result, the customer proximity and the flow of information manage to keep inventory levels to a minimum according to their business model.

Source: www.inditex.com/www.expansion.com.

Rolls-Royce

Rolls-Royce offers a clear example of servitization. Rolls-Royce manufactures engines and for some years has offered a service package whereby customers pay by the hour according to the amount of time an engine is in flight.

This is a significant change from the traditional business models used by manufacturers, in which the manufacturer sells a product and then charges for repair work as often as necessary. In such a model, manufacturers ultimately benefit from unreliable products that need further repairs, a poor fix for customers.

With the TotalCare® service package that Rolls-Royce offers to airlines, the engines are rented to customers. Rolls-Royce monitors engine data to predict potential maintenance problems, meaning that maintenance work is only carried out when necessary. This saves costs on unnecessary maintenance work and reduces the need for unplanned maintenance and engine downtime.

The increased alignment between customer and manufacturer needs that this service enables has had proven business benefits for Rolls-Royce, which has been covering most of its engines with its service package since 2001.

Source: www.rolls roycemotorcars.com/en_GB/home.html/www.aston.ac.uk/.

Caterpillar

Caterpillar provides another strong example of a servitized manufacturing company, offering a portfolio of services beyond production.

One of these services is Cat® Product Link, a remote monitoring and monitoring service. This service provides customers with updates on equipment location and component preventive maintenance monitoring to extend component life and reduce the need for downtime.

Caterpillar monitors equipment remotely, using data sent from Caterpillar vehicles to help make decisions that optimize performance.

Source: www.caterpillar.com/ www.aston.ac.uk/.

Xerox

Another successful manufacturing company now offering advanced services is Xerox. Originally known for copiers, Xerox now positions itself as a business management and process company. Today, more than half of Xerox's business comes from services.

In recent years, Xerox has diversified into offering document production and publishing, document management, and business process outsourcing services. Examples of services in practice include providing Hertz with learning solutions that include curriculum content, administration, and student support services. For Siemens Italia, Xerox created a digital archive and interface to improve document control and reduce waste and paper use.

Source: https://atyourservice.blogs.xerox.com/.

www.emeraldgrouppublishing.com/opinion-and-blog/what-servitization-manufacturing-a-quick-introduction.

Application Exercise

Adding a Service to the Integral Value Chain of a Productive Manufacturing Activity

Purpose

The following application exercise seeks to strengthen the knowledge about the servitization process by practicing the valuation tree in the integral value chain of a well-known business of interest or the analysis of the integral value chain of a product selected from the categories (23) of **manufacturing industries** contained in the United Nations International Standard Industrial Classification of all economic activities (ISIC), described in Chapter 2.

This exercise consists of two phases:

1. Select the integral value chain of a productive manufacturing activity of your interest or make the selection of an ISIC category of the productive activities of **manufacturing industries**.

2. Following the evaluation process of the integral chain of the selected productive activity, identify and base a service to be added as a result of the company's servitization strategy.

Outcome

Service addition project of the servitization strategy.

Final Acknowledgment

Upon completing this application exercise, the reader will have acquired sufficient knowledge of the evaluation process of the integral chain of a productive activity that will enable him to skillfully and effectively approach a servitization strategy.

CHAPTER 3

Service Compliance Management

The assurance of the service delivery in accordance with the value proposition, the user/customer demand, and the encounter experience is an essential matter in the management and outcome. It is to ensure that the agreed attributes are met with their superior value (excellence) and the user approval with maximum satisfaction. These compliance commitments define the link between service and end user, and set up a reliable, effective, and long-term relationship, as well as the branding construction and its positioning in the user mind as it is postulated by the discipline of marketing.

Servimetry is the term associated with the concept of Servilogy, conceived and developed in this work to mean the application of principles, knowledge, methodologies, and tools in measuring the management and performance of the service and the relationship with the user/customer.

Compliance management as a strategic process for ensuring the proper service delivery is an organizational logistical support formed by the set of activities and components used in the provision and confirmation of an agreed value. It is systemic and bimodal in its approach to service and aimed at strengthening quality, consistency, and trust, as well as satisfaction and relationship with the end user. Its analysis and treatment allow the specific objective of measuring compliance with the shared value proposition from the user's perspective. It can be modeled and managed according to the type or nature of the service delivered and with the possibility of being endorsed by an independent entity.

The servitization process entails in its development, the design of a strategic management model to ensure compliance with the delivery phase, the meeting point, the interaction, the experience, and the probable *attraction* of the added service.

Service Compliance Management Pattern

There are several standard references related to information, activity, and technology, for the design of a compliance management system (ITIL4, ISO/IEC20000-1: 2018, COBIT, eTOM, etc.) that can be adaptable to the peculiarities of each organization. However, the immaterial nature of the service, its heterogeneous nature, and the active participation of the user in the experience of value co-creation give rise to the particular *confection* of a pattern of fulfillment appropriate to their distinctive quality.

In this context, the service compliance management process distinguishes three phases:

Service Code

It is the set of principles and values, policies, norms, and business guidelines that are binding on the service proposal: user profile, delivery strategy, user encounter and experience, relevant instrumentation and measurement process, and service audit. The provisions of this code, aimed at planning, activities, operations, performance, and accountability for compliance, govern the personnel behavior at all levels of the organization, as well as its associates, allies, and related parties.

This service regulation conforms specifications such as:

(a) **Service principles.** The set of beliefs and values that define the company commitment, guide, and regulate the provision of service to the internal and external organization user: quality of service, responsibility and compliance in delivery, transparency in interaction and communication, and so on. The heterogeneous nature of service and the user's expectation define the relevant attributes of the service's value proposition.

(b) **Service policy.** It establishes the guidelines and procedures that describe and govern the commitment, performance, and compliance of the organization in its service offering. Define service essential elements such as:
- Know the needs and expectations of the user and always give them the highest priority.
- Maintain a positive, attentive, and cordial attitude during the performance at the encounter point and interaction with the user.

- Adapt the service system to the user requests and expectations.
- Ensure to the user through the engineering and architecture of the service, an environment of convenience, comfort, and safety.
- Attend with decisive character, promptness, diligence and impartiality, the dissatisfaction and inconvenience of the user.

(c) **Service performance scorecard.** It is the organizational management instrument for measuring the performance and evolution of the activity, the objectives, and outcomes of the company's service through the establishment of benchmarks and key performance indicators (KPI). The distinctive character of the service business compared to the manufacturing one leads to the identification of the difference between both processes to empower and create the appropriate and effective service management scorecard.

The service process presents different dimensions and attributes in relation to manufacturing companies, particularly in regard to people, operations, and artifacts. The people-oriented service process and its reason for being as a business are defined by the interaction of creating memorable experiences for the end user.

What attributes that characterize the service business are necessary to know in order to create and institute a set of KPI and a service-balanced scorecard?

The following chart shows the characteristic attributes of the service business.

Table 3.1 Attributes of the service business

Factor	Attributes
Input	Data, information, knowledge
Supplier	Few with intense bonding
User	Look for results, solutions, experiences. Participates in the delivery of the service, performance is an intangible complex to measure, etc.
Process	Sequence of integrating activities of people, approaches, methods, materials, equipment, and tools.
Outcome	Experiences that create the result: satisfaction, solution, bonding, trust, etc.

From this distinctive perspective, the creation of a service-balanced scorecard focuses on defining the principles and criteria for measuring performance and identifying and establishing the key success indicators for its measurement process and subsequent action.

This activity distinguishes the service mode and the five phases in the value chain:

1. The commitment of the organization, company, and business.
2. The employee identification and commitment with the organization and the end user.
3. The excellence or quality level in the operation and delivery process.
4. The end-user experience and satisfaction.
5. The customer connection and trust.

The structure of the service-balanced scorecard serves as a reference instrument for measuring compliance and conformity with the service purposes. It offers a complete vision at the level of (A) user, (B) management, (C) operation, (D) performance, and (E) supplier that are shown as an illustration in Table 3.2.

Measurement of Service Compliance

The process of applying the evaluation methods and instruments from the user's perspective, analysis of the information, interpretation of the results, issuance of the report, and adoption of actions related to compliance and conformity of the service proposal.

Conceptually, the service measurement is based on its intangible nature and the user´s leading role. In this context, the orientation of the verification methods and instruments is directed in contrast to those of manufacturing, outside the company. It is the fulfillment, conformity, satisfaction, and linking of the user's needs and expectations with the value proposition, its implementation, delivery, meeting, and the service experience along with essential correspondence to the service business success and sustainability.

The availability of reference methods and instruments for measuring service is wide and varied. In this phase of the process, known, proven,

Table 3.2 Service performance indicators

Vision	Objective	Indicator	Measurement (*)
User	Satisfy	Compliance Satisfaction Dissatisfaction Defection Recovery	Servqual/E-S-Qual The Kano model
	Experience	Experience Satisfaction Dissatisfaction	NPS/CES
	Trust	Retention Loyalty Recurrence Reference	NPS
Management	Lead	Leadership Strategic direction	
	Grow	New services New customers Innovation Sustainability Competitiveness	NPS
Operation	Execute	Efficiency Quality Effectiveness Productivity Capacity Convenience Comfort Process	ISO standards
	Improve	Technology Innovation	
Performance	Deliver	Performance Commitment	
	Comply	Compliance Achievement Outcome Solution Trust	Various performance evaluation tools
Supplier	Deliver Comply	Reliability Compliance Relationship Responsibility Logistic Prestige (reputation) Quality	Various performance evaluation tools

(*) Models and tools

and frequently used instruments are presented by companies in the key areas of management, operation, and performance.

1. **The Servqual[1]/E-S-Qual[2] model.** It is one of the best known and applied tools in measuring the quality-of-service business, from the user´s perception and expectation. It offers a version for assessing the quality of the face-to-face service and another for the virtual or electronic service delivered over the Internet.

   In the face-to-face model, the quality of the service is conceptualized in 21 questions grouped into five (5) dimensions: reliability, responsibility, assurance, empathy, and tangible that are adaptable to the situations of each evaluated service and described in the table below:

Table 3.3 Servqual dimensions

Dimension	Description
1. Reliability	Ability to execute and deliver the service on time, in the same way and without defects.
2. Responsibility	Willingness and responsiveness
3. Assurance	Competence to provide the service
4. Empathy	Flexibility to place oneself in the user's position
5. Tangibles	Physical appearance of personnel, facilities, and communication

Source: Parasuraman, A., V. Ziethaml, and L. Berry. 1988. "SERVQUAL: A Multiple-Item Scale for Measuring Consumer Perceptions of Service Quality." *Journal of Retailing* 62, no. 1, pp. 12–40.

In the electronic model, the user assesses the service quality from the perspective of how the website efficiently and effectively facilitates the search, purchase, and delivery of the service. This is done through a questionnaire of 11 questions grouped into 3 dimensions: contact, responsiveness, and compensation for incidents and noncompliance.

Table 3.4 shows the evaluated attributes.

2. **The Kano model.[3]** It is a tool for identifying, classifying, and measuring the relationship between the attributes of a product and the degree of satisfaction they produce for the consumer. This model

Table 3.4 E-S-Qual dimensions

Attribute	Description
Reliability	Correct technical operation of the site and the accuracy of service promises (have items in stock, deliver what was ordered, deliver when promised), billing, and product information.
Responsiveness	Promptness of response and ability to solve problems and resolve questions and concerns.
Access	Ease to access the site quickly and connecting with the company when necessary.
Flexibility	Choice of payment methods, shipping, purchase, search, and return of items.
Ease to navigate	The site contains functions that help users to easily find what they need; it has good search functionality and allows the user to move easily and quickly from one side to the other of the pages.
Efficiency	The site is easy to use, is structured correctly, and requires minimal information to be entered by the user.
Assurance/trust	The trust that the user feels in their interaction with the site based on the prestige of the site, the products, or services it sells, and the clear and truthful information presented.
Security/privacy	Degree to which the user believes that the site is safe from intrusions and that personal information is protected.
Price knowledge	Degree to which the user can determine the shipping price, the total price, and the comparative prices during the purchase process.
Site aesthetics	Appearance of the site
Customization/ personalization	How much and how easily the site can be adapted to the preferences, stories, and ways of buying of individual users.

Source: Zeithaml, V.A., A. Parasuraman, and A. Malhotra. 2005. "E-S-Qual: A Multiple-Item Scale for Assessing Electronic Service Quality." *Journal of Service Research* 7, no. 3, pp. 213–233.

results in theory for product development by focusing on distinctive specifications, rather than initially focusing on consumer needs. It establishes five quality categories to catalog customer preferences:

- **Reverse or Rejection:** Characteristics of the product perceived as negative and that produce rejection.
- **Indifferent:** The product attributes that do not have a favorable or unfavorable impact on customer satisfaction.
- **Basic or expected (Satisfactors):** Minimum attributes of a product that the consumer expects and that causes dissatisfaction if they are not there.

- **Desired (Unsatisfying):** Attributes requested of a product and that significantly influence consumer or user satisfaction. They are indicators of competitiveness.
- **Attractive (Delightful):** Attributes that surprise the customer which he also values. Their absence does not impact customer satisfaction.

Source: Kano, N., N. Seraku, F. Takahashi, and S. Tsuji. 1984. "Attractive Quality and Must-Be Quality." *Hinshitsu: The Journal of the Japanese Society for Quality Control* 14, no. 2, pp. 39–48.

3. **Recommendation index:** better known as NPS, net promoter score. It is a method/indicator for measuring customer satisfaction and loyalty oriented by the answer to the question about the probability of recommending, advising, or referring a product (service, company, business, brand, event, etc.) to another person (friend, relative, etc.).[4]

   The response on a scale of 0–10 allows the identification of three (3) categories of clients: detractor (0–6), passive (7–8), and promoter (9–10).

   It is considered a method of generalized use, simple, and an accurate indicator of the experience lived at the encounter place, be it face-to-face or digital.

4. **Effort index:** CES, customer effort score, is a metric that estimates the degree of effort of a user (time and energy) to manage and achieve their purpose (buy, use a service, request information, or solve a situation) each time they access and interact with a company or brand. It is measured by the question: How easy is it for you to achieve what you require from this company? Using a numerical rating scale of 1–7, where 1 indicates the greatest probability of repurchase, increased spending, and user recommendation, while a score of 7 shows the most difficult or negative experience. A score of 7 also indicates the true probability of not only not returning but of commenting on it in their immediate environment as well as on social networks with its undesirable consequences.

   The logic behind the ease of the experience is that the less effort, the greater the possibility of winning the loyalty of the user.[5]

5. **Customer experience index:** As its name indicates, it measures the *experience* of the user with the encounter, interaction, and comfort

of the service. Having a holistic vision of the customer's perception in the service encounter implies estimating a set of variables, some of them already considered in the previous sections, such as satisfaction, NPS, CES, retention, desertion (churn), customer value, and so on.

In this context, emotions are a central factor to consider. The importance of emotions is in decision-making and the customer bond creation which are keys to customer loyalty.

In this area, the arrangement of systems, models, and tools is varied and extensive, starting from Robert Plutchik's "wheel of emotions"[6] to Forrester's CX index,[7] one of the best known and most authorized on the topic.

The Compliance Assurance

The managerial verification process between the organization's commitment and the service performance considers how the established principles correspond to the company's governance scheme. The results and recommendations are reported for continuous monitoring and assurance.

In this phase, possible barriers to satisfactory fulfillment of the service commitment are recorded, analyzed, and managed: unforeseen events or events that occurred during the service process. These possible barriers could be difficulties that prevent the provision of the service, additional requests, or requests outside the service proposal and inconveniences in accessing the service.

Application Exercise

Management of Service Compliance

Purpose

The following application exercise seeks to consolidate knowledge about the process and instruments for ensuring performance and service compliance and the experience with the user.

Select one of the tools described in the previous chapter and apply it to a known service of your interest.

(a) Design the application instrument or use an available format
(b) Validate the instrument for understanding and accuracy
(c) Select at least 10 service users
(d) Apply instrument, tabulate, and analyze information. Prepare a report and be prepared for presentation.

Outcome

Appropriation of knowledge and development of skills for the management of service compliance assurance.

Final Acknowledgment

Upon completing this application exercise, the reader will have acquired sufficient knowledge of instruments for measuring service delivery, performance, and experience; as well as acquired skills for the management of the assurance of the fulfillment of the service with the user.

CHAPTER 4

Dynamic Capabilities

We desperately need the expertise of those who are educated in the human, cultural and social, as well as computationally.

—Steve Jobs

The management and performance of the added service in the servitization strategy continues to be a challenging process for the leadership of the company. Rethinking the skills required of employees in their selection and training processes will ensure the quality of service, interaction, and relational experience with the user to guarantee the business success. These capabilities are not only focused on technical skills or transactional processes but also in soft, transversal, or socioemotional skills, which enable the service professional to interact and relate effectively with their peers or others.

Identified as socioemotional or professional T-shaped skills, currently highly appreciated by companies, are the component or integration in an entity or entity of specialized knowledge in an area (vertical bar) with the transversal skills (horizontal bar) that they give an open, global profile that is very easy to adapt.

This professional, also known by the title of *service engineer* or *STEEP professional*, for its acronym in English, is the basis of training today and the service and manufacturing industry, and understands the STEEP factors: **S**ocial, **T**echnological, **E**conomic, **E**nvironmental, and **P**olitical.[1, 2]

Occupational and Service Management Skills

Advances in the knowledge and practice of the service have established a set of generally accepted standard capabilities for its effective performance and management. These range from the actions of routine, habitual, or unskilled work to activities of high complexity and great personal autonomy.

These standard competencies are known, applied, and periodically evaluated by companies and brands of recognized prestige in the market in their selection and training processes for their personnel.[3, 4]

Professional Performance Skills

The effective performance of a service is based on the knowledge and development of five factors:

Principles of Service

Provide reliable customer service. Three key components make up the development of this competence:

Theoretical Foundation.   What knowledge is necessary?

An academic and multidisciplinary research effort to seek, develop, and promote knowledge of the nature of services, improve, create, and innovate in service, resulted in a set of theories and methods that have given rise to the principles, approaches, methods, and tools that allow understanding and managing the process of value co-creation in business. These foundations enunciated under the denomination of Service Science and exposed throughout this work serve the valid purpose of education and training for the service.[5]

Organizational context.   What purpose to serve?

The ability to know, identify, assume, and fulfill the company value promises with the user: the concept of service, organizational principles and values, policies, standards, processes, and delivery procedures of the service proposal.

Environment/Experience of the Service Encounter.   How do you act in creating a positive user experience?

The knowledge of the physical conditions and circumstances, the emotional modulation, and the adequate performance in the interaction process of the service delivery constitutes the essential elements for a positive and satisfactory experience with the user.

Image and Impression of the Service

What elements should be of high consideration?

Give the customer a good personal, company and service impression. The image and the first good impression are, in addition to the presentation letter of a service, a differentiating element (branding) and an integrating axis of socioemotional capabilities (service culture). They are a source of reputation, growth, and profit for the company. The characteristic competencies to project an image and generate a positive first impression of a service are personal presentation (image, presence, and aesthetics) and modulation of socioemotional skills (attitude, empathy, communication, etc.).

Fulfillment of the Service Commitment

How do you fulfill the promise of value?

Developing the ability to comply with the user request means knowing how to identify and define a strategy and a service delivery system. In section D, systematicity and transversality of the service (Chapter 1) and the management of service compliance (Chapter 4) that develops the process of assuring delivery and compliance with the company's commitment, this process is addressed, and the aspects are detailed that serve as a guide for the development or strengthening of this competence.

Management of Critical Situations With Users

How do you deal with customer complaints, requests, and problems?

The ability to recognize, manage, and act with resolution aptitude in the face of potential conflict situations in the service with the user is a key issue for perception and an opportunity to improve the service, as well as a personal professional challenge. In this context, the contents of the training programs emphasize socioemotional skills. The mastery and deployment of these skills are put to test in each service encounter and determine the difference in the user experience.

Development of the User Relationship

How do you create effective, productive, and lasting relationships?

Interaction with the users and the search for new and innovative ways to *delight* them are the key to a long, effective, and productive relationship. Developing this personnel ability strengthens the potential of linking the user with the service and the company, creates loyalty bonds, and establishes a source of sustainable competitive advantage for the business.

The following table displays in detail the five standard occupational skills for the direct performance of the service with the user.

Table 4.1 Occupational performance capabilities

Occupational standard	Capabilities
Fundamentals of service	a. Know and understand the conceptual foundations of the service b. Know and understand the company's service proposal c. Provide the service following the principles and regulations of the organization
Image and impression	a. Give the customer a good personal, company and service impression b. Attend and process service information request c. Fulfill the promise to the user d. "Customize" the service e. Go the extra mile and exceed expectations f. Communicate effectively with the user via written, telephone, or internet g. Attend and treat the user with cordiality, promptness, and respect h. Identify and promote additional services or products i. Use the service as a competitive tool
Fulfillment of the commitment	a. Provide consistent and reliable service to the user b. Provide a service that fulfills the promise to the user c. Recognize diversity and serve it while providing the service d. Develop and maintain a safe, healthy, and enjoyable service environment e. Plan, organize, and control service operations f. Evaluate the quality of the service
Management of critical situations	a. Develop trust at the level of the service provided b. Process and solve potentially conflictive situations (complaints, requests, and problems) c. Analyze and select the best option to solve a situation d. Implement the solution e. Monitor and evaluate potential risks
Develop relationships with the user	a. Ensure the satisfaction of needs and exceed user expectations b. Build the relationship between the user and the company

Source: ADAPTED AND WITH PERMISSION of the Institute of Customer Service. 2006. Overviews of National Occupational Standards in Customer Service at NVQ/SVQ Units at Levels 2, 3 and Level 4, UK.

Managerial Performance Skills

What must leaders and managers do to inspire the organization to focus on users and achieve excellence in service delivery?

A look at the organizations that have succeeded in developing and maintaining a reputation for excellence in service serves as a reference and guide for companies in their quest to add value to their business through the adoption and implementation of a servitization strategy. This observation shows that the main components of care are: a clear service culture, a distinctive service personality, committed talent, and user-centered systems, all under a single holistic approach.

The impact of these developments on the company's employees is considerable. It strengthens the recognition that the key to making a real difference in service performance standards is in knowledge, skill, attitude, and personal judgment.

Likewise, often the people in contact and direct customer service positions have been hired, managed, and recognized according to their ability to manage specific and internally oriented activities and processes of the organization. This has changed and organizational leadership has adopted a talent endowment, training, and development approach that enables it to:

- Apply well-established behavioral skills in such a way that they allow individual and satisfactory service to each user, be able to co-create an environment for a positive experience, and identify additional service or product opportunities.
- Solve, proactively and reactively, potential conflict situations based on the ability to properly identify and interpret critical service issues.
- Appreciate "the integral vision" of the service experience to make better decisions, understanding the consequences of their actions for the company.
- Identify opportunities to improve procedures and systems.
- Interact in a cordial and concerted way with their peers and other collaborators to make the learning and experience shared and enriching. Also, that they know and stay updated with the products and services of the company.

This direction occupies a central role in managers to make sense of all these incentives and create the environment in which workers are continuously stimulated to make the service add value to the business of quality, productivity, competitiveness, and profit.

Studies carried out for the identification, development, and validation of standards for managerial positions in business service indicate that businesses are in search of a significantly improved user/customer approach by managers, whatever their level is in the organization. This implies that all managers need to:

- Demonstrate leadership and develop the conviction that the company and its people can achieve not only what they say about the importance of their customer orientation but also their actions are based on a firmly articulated set of values.
- Build relationships with clients and allies that guarantee permanent loyalty.
- Challenge the current conception of service, follow its evolution, and be receptive to new contributions that will base continuous improvement in the provision of services.
- Support and encourage those who have responsibility in the process of encounter, delivering and bonding with the user.

There are additional challenges for the growing number of managers with explicit responsibilities in the provision and allocation of resources, particularly the human one due to its criticality in the user experience.

- Create an environment in which people, especially those who are in direct contact with the user, are encouraged to achieve greater attainments.
- Advise and support people in the internalization of the principles and values of the organization and stimulate the development of personal efficiency.
- Encourage people to value, commit, and take care of their own learning and development.
- Model the culture and profile of the best performance in the encounter, contact, and direct interaction with the user.

- Demonstrate perseverance in innovation and constant improvement in the provision of services.
- Understand the economics of the business and contribute to the service strategy.

The chart below illustrates the standard managerial capabilities for service management.

Table 4.2 Management performance capabilities

Management performance	Capabilities
1. Cooperate with the design and development of the company service strategy or specific area	a. Know and analyze the company business strategy b. Cooperate in identifying the user´s needs and expectations c. Cooperate in the identification of good practices and trends in services d. Identify and propose key factors or components of a service strategy
2. Cooperate in training and development of service talent	a. Cooperate in the identification of training and development needs b. Cooperate in the design and development of training c. Participate in the process of training and permanent updating d. Evaluate the impact and contribution of the training
3. Plan, organize, and control service operations	a. Plan operations b. Implement projects and operational plans c. Ensure that service operations comply with the established requirements d. Manage situations and problems related to service operational activities
4. Establish and maintain a safe, healthy, and effective work environment	a. Evaluate the work environment to identify factors that affect health, safety, and effectiveness b. Reduce health and safety risks c. Maintain an effective work environment
5. Manage the use of physical resources	a. Plan the use of resources b. Obtain physical resources c. Ensure the availability of supplies d. Monitor the use of physical resources
6. Cooperate in the management of technology facilities and operations	a. Monitor and control the operation of telecommunications facilities b. Identify problems related to the operations of telecommunications facilities c. Identify solutions for operational problems d. Implement solutions for operational problems
7. Assess the quality of service	a. Plan how to measure the service and establish performance indicators b. Apply tools and analyze information about service c. Analyze and report the results on the service quality

(Continues)

Table 4.2 (Continued)

8. Cooperate in the design and implementation of improvements in the service quality	a. Cooperate to develop and strengthen service standards and specifications b. Cooperate in the design of improvements for the customer c. Plan the incorporation of service improvements. d. Manage the incorporation of service improvements e. Evaluate service improvements
9. Manage referred customer complaints	a. Investigate referred customer complaints b. Take action to solve referred customer complaints c. Consistently identify referred customer complaints and propose changes to policies and procedures
10. Develop and maintain effective relationships with customers	a. Establish effective customer relationships b. Develop and maintain effective customer relationships
11. Promote and support user service	a. Promote the importance and benefits of user service b. Advise and report on matters related to the service
12. Working as a team to strengthen the service performance	a. Guide and improve the work of the staff b. Promote effective collaborative relationships between the members and work areas of the organization c. Promote collaborative relationships with coworkers
13. Capitalize own resources management	a. Stay updated and in constant training to improve your own performance. b. Manage the time and resources allocated to achieve the established outcomes.

SOURCE: ADAPTED AND WITH PERMISSION of the Institute of Customer Service. 2006. Overviews of National Occupational Standards in Customer Service at NVQ/SVQ Units at Levels 2,3 and Level 4, UK.

The Services Professional

The servitization process is considered as adding value to manufacturing companies through the integration of service activities or related to the business value chain. It breaks into the dynamics of the organization and encourages the reconsideration of its dynamic capabilities, particularly those related to the skills of human talent.

Is there a distinctive and relevant factor of human talent in the performance of the service that determines the success in the value creation interaction?

Let's think about the socioemotional capabilities (soft skills) that, being inherent to human action and required or not by all work activities, are decisive for the satisfactory result of service management due to their high level of intensity and variability of the environment. For its part, job performance in the manufacturing company is predominantly focused on hard skills or scientific, technological, engineering, and mathematical competencies (STEM Education Model) where the level of intensity required of soft skills is lower depending on the limited environment and little variable internal interaction of the organization.

Talent in Services

The academic approach or training for performance in the service industry forms, in addition to natural talent, a category of knowledge and skills with a differentiated emphasis on two aspects: emotional and interpersonal skills, distinctive in relation to workers in the manufacturing industry. The emotional ones are related to the ability of a person to autonomously modulate the expression of his or her emotions, while interpersonal skills are formed by the set of behaviors and habits necessary for appropriate interaction and collaborative work with others and with the diverse environment.

These *soft skills*, a distinctive factor in organizational performance and a key to success in the service business, demand a strategic approach in the manufacturing business:

- Identification and development of the weakest soft skills in the organization.
- Selection, training, and retention of collaborators, through carefully defined support mechanisms as in the case of customer groups (segmentation).

The following table, adapted from Working with Emotional Intelligence by Daniel Goleman,[6] illustrates the main socioemotional capacities with their attributes in the business environment that impact the high performance of the service and that it is convenient for every business to promote:

The cultivation and practice of these dynamic and differentiating capabilities strengthen the organizational culture of performance and give

Table 4.3 Socioemotional capabilities

Skill	Attribute
EMOTIONAL	Self-control
SELF KNOWLEDGE • Awareness • Self-appraisal • Confidence	Internal states, preferences, resources, and own intuitions • Own emotions and their effects • Own forces and limits • Certainty of value and own powers
SELF-MODERATION • Self-control • Reliability • Rigor • Adaptability • Innovation	Modulate internal states, impulses, and own resources • Harmful emotions and impulses • Practice of honesty and integrity • Responsibility for personal performance • Flexibility for change • Willingness for new ideas, approaches, and information
MOTIVATION • Achievement • Commitment • Initiative • Optimism	Emotional inclination that guides/facilitates achievement • Effort toward excellence • Assume the purposes of the group or organization • Willingness to seize opportunities • Persistent in the face of obstacles and setbacks
SOCIAL EMPATHY • Understanding • Support for • To serve • Diversity • Political consciousness	Relationship management skills Identification with the needs, feelings, and interests of others • Perception, understanding, and interest in other people's feelings and perspectives • Help and promote the development of others • Co-create value with the user to satisfy their needs and expectations • Cultivate opportunities through personal differences • Interpret the emotional current of a person or group and its relationship to power
SOCIAL SKILLS • Influence • Communication • Problem solving • Leadership • Catalyst for change • Establish links • Collaboration and cooperation • Team skills	Ability to induce desirable responses in the other • Persuasiveness • Ability to listen actively and issue clear and convincing messages • Negotiate and resolve differences • Inspire and guide individuals or groups • Willingness to initiate or manage change • Create, maintain, and strengthen bonds • Work with others to achieve shared purposes • Create synergy to achieve collective purposes

Source: ADAPTED AND WITH PERMISSION of Penguin Random House LLC. Goleman, D. 1998. Working with Emotional Intelligence, Batam Dell.

the service professional, active in the design, management and operation of the service. A multidisciplinary profile, by integrating socioemotional skills with categories of knowledge, made up of adequate proportion of scientific-technical, economic-business, and cultural-social knowledge.

This fact in a manufacturing environment raises rethinking the selection and training of employees to respond to the demands of new additions to the integral business value chain.

This means enhancing business benefits through the development of human resources strategies:

- Investment in human development vs. staff turnover and training costs.
- The positioning of the service through the development of qualities in the employees that are more effective than their competition counterparts.
- Eliminate unnecessary emphasis on rigid policies or support systems that interfere with employees' ability to solve customer problems.
- Quality improvement by reducing individual judgment in the delivery process and service experience.

Application Exercise

Capabilities for Selection and Training

Objective

Strengthen knowledge and develop skills to identify capabilities required for the performance of service positions in the company.

Instructions

Considering the capabilities for service performance developed in the previous chapter:

(a) Select a professional and a managerial position from a known service of interest to you.
(b) Identify for each of the positions, the key occupational and managerial performance capabilities.
(c) Identify and outline the key socioemotional capabilities for those positions in the selected service.
(d) Prepare the professional profile required for the two positions identified.

Outcome

Appropriation of knowledge on occupational and managerial capacities for performance in services and development of skills for the selection and training of prospects and collaborators.

Final Acknowledgment

Upon completing this application exercise, the reader will have acquired sufficient knowledge about the occupational, managerial, and socioemotional capacities to perform in the services, and will be able to put them into practice in the selection and training of candidates and active collaborators of a company.

CHAPTER 5

Innovation and Sustainability

The concepts of innovation and sustainability give projection to the service and constitute real challenges for the permanence of the businesses in the market. The ever-changing user expectations and the highly competitive business environment demand from companies and their leadership creative and innovative responses contribute to their stability and continuous growth.

The cases of innovative and sustainable services such as Uber, Cabify, Lyft, and so forth in the transportation network company sector and Airbnb in hotels and hospitality, and so on, are known as well as the potential for innovation in the services identified in each phase of the manufacturing process:[1, 2]

- **Services associated with the consumer**: the role of the customer, the delivery of the product, and the point of consumption.
- **Services associated with the product** and related to its nature and presentation.
- **Services associated with production**: technology, skills, operations, organization, and so on.
- **Services associated with the market**: types of entities or markets, regulatory and marketing matters.

These purposes permeate the servitization strategy, take shape, and define its own perspective and entity.

A Model of Innovation

The servitization construct is conceptually an innovation model by referring to the transformation process from a product-centered business form to an integrated system of products and services that proposes strategic and competitive benefits to the company. From this perspective, servitization involves challenges and the first is in the purpose of achieving the visualization of new value proposals that impact the integral chain of business profit.[3, 4] In this regard, it has been possible to develop schemes that facilitate the identification of service types and roles, as well as axes of innovation in the development of strategies in product companies, considering when these and their business structures complement, replace, or create products and services.

Innovation Axis by Service

This classification of services guides the action of the innovation process by separating them into three groups:

(a) **Associated services:** They facilitate the sale and use of the product without altering its functionality. They are the services of operation, technical support, maintenance, mentoring, training, and among others. They are inherent or added to the product and can be offered by the company or a commercial partner.

(b) **Adaptation services:** They are integrated into the product to extend its functionality or provide it with new uses. These services are commonly known under the concept of personalization or customization and require a greater exchange of knowledge between the manufacturer and its user/consumer.

(c) **Substitute services:** These services replace the purchase of the product, and the consumer mainly pays for its use. Also known as *Advanced Services*, they represent a level of evolution in the servitization strategy of manufacturing companies and constitute the *Product as a Service* or *Product-Service System* model (PAAS and PSS, respectively), today of wide interest and application in the sector.

The *Product as a Service* is also an economic model different from the traditional linear *buy-spend-discard* model, where the consumer discards it when he no longer needs the product. In the context of the circular economic archetype (circular economy), the disposable product returns to the producer where it can be recycled or given a new use or application.

This *circular connection* gives the PAAS/PSS model a significant value for companies that seek to boost the profitability of their products, strengthen relationships with customers, and launch new sustainable business lines.

Well-known companies in the manufacturing sectors benefit from the PAAS/PSS model, such as Xerox, Hp and Lexmark, Rolls-Royce and General Electric, Philips, Apple, John Deere, among others.

Innovation Axis by Product Life Cycle

Another axis of innovation in the servitization process is the analysis of the stages of the product or industry life cycle. This opportunity to adapt services is presented, previously taking into consideration at the beginning of the life cycle that the level of cost and uncertainty related to the product and the market are high, and that as the phases of the life cycle advance toward their maturity, these conditions diminish, and the services acquire more relevance.

In the case of replacement services, although they may arise in the initial phase of the cycle as in cases of extreme uncertainty, they are more frequent in the maturity stage, when companies seek to expand the market to attract new customers who cannot pay or they do not consider the purchase of the product useful, profitable, or of interest. These options depend on the type of industrial environment of the company. From the standpoint of Schumpeter's Creative Destruction theory,[5] companies choose product-oriented services in industrial settings, while customer-oriented services are more sought-after in-service settings. This is because product companies do not necessarily follow the product-service continuum.

These services respond to requests and opportunities that one faces in the life cycle of the industry. Additionally, they aim to complement and leverage each other and expand product sales.[6, 7] Consequently, various service strategies result in different modes and levels of servitization, which in turn require appropriate reconfigurations of the business model.[8]

Innovation Axis by Company Size

Servitization as a business innovation model is nourished by valid and effective innovation models that help to visualize and holistically identify the manufacturing process to analyze its possibilities in terms of adding value as services. The Business Innovation Assessment, a proposed logical scheme to guide the identification of innovation opportunities, serves as a reference for this purpose:

This framework identifies five key areas with its main points of search for opportunities in a business innovation process from its initial value proposition and all the way down to the end customer: (1) user/consumer, (2) portfolio, (3) manufacturing, (4) marketing, and (5) meeting place:

1. **User/Customer**

   Understanding the user and consumer of the company's products and services in its broadest dimension is key to success in identifying innovation opportunities. The effective analysis of this area of innovation in its more extensive concept (user, consumer, and market) and based on what really matters and influences giving, collaborating, or purchasing decisions. This understanding allows the company the opportunity of discovering new customers, segments, or unmet needs, wants, expectations. Two main drivers of innovation are highlighted here:

   (a) **The Interaction Experience:** The user experience at every moment of their interaction with the business at any meeting point. Innovating here means rethinking the company's approach and contact with its customers as well as its environment. Data analytics, research like focus groups, in-depth interviews, social media analysis, and feedback from existing customers are all helpful for that purpose.

(b) **Value-added:** The enhancement in quality, service, value, or extent that the company creates for its products or services and is perceived as important, useful, or beneficial by customers. Expanding the ability to co-create value from interactions with its customers in an array of sources and without developing sophisticated and expensive methods or systems.

2. **Portfolio**

The set of all items (products and services) offered by the company. The analysis of this innovation phase provides the opportunity to discover and develop new products and services that are valuable to customers. Two key factors of innovation to explore are as follows:

(a) **Model:** The archetype used by the company to design and develop a diverse, derivative, and differentiated value proposition of products and services. This often-underestimated factor is a potential source of considerable value creation. A good reference in this regard is the pattern used by the automotive industry in its variety and endless designs.

(b) **Solutions:** It is the customization, integration, and information of a product or service that solves the situation or problem of a user/consumer. The variety and depth of the company's assortment is a good example of value creation in this factor.

3. **Manufacturing**

The scaffolding of processes and activities used to carry out the operations of the company. Finding the best way to perform more efficient operations, with higher quality or with more punctual delivery, is an opportunity offered by this phase and it has been the basis for the success of many companies that have taken advantage of it. This stage offers three central factors for innovation:

(a) **Structure:** It refers to the organizational structure of the company. The way in which the company aligns its associations, roles, and responsibilities with its collaborators and allies. Innovating along this factor means rethinking the scope of the company's activities, as well as redefining the roles, responsibilities, and incentives of the different business units and people.

(b) **Supply chain:** The network (activities, people, entities, information, and resources) between the company and its suppliers to produce and distribute products and services to the final user/consumer. It represents a sequence of steps that serve to scrutinize sources of innovation. The company's ability to streamline the flow of information through this sequence of steps results in innovating its structure or improving the collaboration of its participants.

4. **Marketing**

The activity, processes, and agents for creating, communicating, delivering, and exchanging value propositions for customers. Market intelligence and database analysis make this axis of business activity a valid, effective, and large source of information and communication for innovation in the company.

5. **Meeting place**

Channels and meeting points that a company uses to offer its portfolio to the market as well as the user/consumer where they can get their products or services. Innovation in this area involves creating new outlets or using existing ones in creative ways. Particular attention must be paid to the convenience and comfort of the user at the meeting point. The service environment is key to success in user experience, satisfaction, and trust.

(a) **Networking:** The connection of the company's products and services with its users or consumers. This connection when converted into a franchise results in a competitive advantage for the business. Innovating in this area means strengthening and expanding the network to increase the value of the company's offerings.

(b) **Branding:** The symbols, words, signs, or distinctive by which a company communicates its promise of value to users/consumers. Extending or leveraging your brand creatively is the way to innovate in this factor, associated with marketing strategies.

Assessing each of these main business components in terms of innovation requires a holistic and exhaustive vision, considering the user/consumer needs and expectations, the attributes of each product and service based on their distinctive qualities, as well as their contributions, and its organizational structure and operations.

Innovation Metrics

How to measure innovation in the company?

The management of innovation in business requires, in addition to identifying potential areas of innovation, defining, and communicating the appropriate evaluation metrics. Chapter 3 on service compliance management describes a general set of indicators relevant to their performance, taking as a reference the well-known model of the four perspectives: The Balanced Scorecard by the authors Kaplan and Norton.[9, 10] Based on the innovation axes of a business, described earlier, a set of indicators are identified and established by way of illustration:

Table 5.1 Innovation metrics

Phase	Indicator
User/consumer	• New customers, segments, or unmet needs • New experiences • Value recovery/recapture methods • New income streams • Novel pricing systems
Portfolio	• New and innovative products and services • Quality and reliability level • Technological application level • Reduction of the product and service development cycle
Manufacturing	• Innovations in production and processes: performance and benefits • Refinement of the supply/delivery model for greater efficiency, higher quality, or faster cycle time • Rethink company activities • Redefine the roles, responsibilities, and incentives of different business units and individuals • Information flow through the supply chain, change its structure, or improve the collaboration of its participants • Technological investment/application level
Marketing	• Reach & Engagement • Actionable ideas (having practical value) • Innovation costs and benefits • Cultural impact
Meeting place	• New points of purchase/meeting • Redesign of existing ones • Improve the network to increase the value of the offering • Extend or take advantage of the brand

A Sustainable Service

The concept of sustainability in practice refers to the integration and reconciliation of environmental, social, and economic values to maintain life in the long term. Its application is common to any process, whatever its nature: product, company, sector, and so on. In this context, servitization is a potential opportunity to incorporate socio-environmental values in the process of co-creation of value with the user by infusing the principle of sustainability in the process of preparation, delivery, and experience of the service.

"Service and the dominant logic of service[11] that drive today's global economy permeate all aspects of daily life and shape social and natural environments." Also, the service activity requires physical and nonphysical resources with potential short- and long-term effects on both a local and global scale. From this perspective, the quality of intangibility and the perishable nature of the service, its cyclical and transformational continuity over time without negatively affecting the natural or social environment, impose the design, development, and delivery of *sustainable services.*

What is a sustainable service?

A sustainable service is understood to be that one that meets the needs and expectations of the user and remains innovative over time without negatively impacting its natural or social environment. Based both on the intelligent and efficient integration of physical and nonphysical resources and on behaving with environmental and social awareness, sustainable service also carries substantial economic benefits.

The adoption of this quality in the servitization process promotes the creation of sustainable services while transforming the user into a permanent agent of sustainability. It is to be observed, as Wolfson[12] points out, that the sustainable service adds in its unidirectional, bidirectional, and partner composition, a cogeneration of direct and indirect values to other users or actors in the process, and to while grounded in the succession of social, environmental, and economic values (sustainability), they approach the concept of ecosystem services, that is, those benefits that people obtain from nature.

A Sustainable Service Model

How to infuse sustainability in the generation of services in the servitization process?

The application of the concept of sustainability in addition to the services of the company's integral value chain is an opportunity to revitalize the mutual connection between sustainability and service. A relationship, that is an integral part of the interaction and a means through which sustainability is produced and delivered, defines a continuity of the service from generation to generation.

Wolfson's sustainable service model,[13] which serves as a reference for the inclusion of the concept of sustainability in the servitization strategy, suggests seven criteria for the design, development, operation, and implementation of a sustainable service; among these, the following stands out:

1. **Sustainable value:** Sustainability must be an essential part in delivering value as well as a service in itself.
2. **Co-creation of value:** The integral process of value co-creation must be included from the service delivery structure and the participation of the user in the interactive process of resources, activities, and capacities.
3. **Total and continuous value:** These qualities must be inclusive and receive due attention.
4. **Life cycle of the value:** All phases of the service life cycle including physical and nonphysical resources must contain the concept of sustainability.
5. **The intangibility of value:** The appropriate solution must be based on an intangible value.

With these criteria in mind, the conceptualization of a sustainable service comprises three phases:

1. **Identify the essential components of the service value chain**
    (a) Identify the value proposition of the service.
    (b) Identify the provider and user of the service.

    (c) Identify and characterize the main operational and technological processes involved in the production of the service from the provider to the end user and how the end user makes use of them.

    (d) Identify and characterize suppliers, supply, indirect users, and interested parties.

    (e) Identify the distinctive attributes (associated values) of the service proposal.

    (f) Identify the resources and capacities required for both the provider and the user of the service.

    (g) Identify the environmental, social, and economic values of the service.

    (h) Identify the responsibilities for the sustainability of each actor in the production, delivery, and use of the service.

2. **Engineering and service project**

    (a) Qualify and quantify the use of physical and nonphysical resources: materials, energy, infrastructure, efforts, information, and knowledge.

    (b) Identify the short- and long-term effects, as well as the local and global impact of the service.

    (c) Qualify and quantify the distribution of resources and tasks between the provider and the user and between the value proposition and the distinctive attributes of the service.

3. **Alternative proposals**

    (a) Identify alternate routes to supply the same solution.

    (b) Identify support services to ensure the sustainability of the service proposal.

    (c) Compare the options by following all the steps, resources, values, and so on.

The Environmental, Social, and Economic Values of the Service

How to identify the sustainability components as values in the service design?

    Knowledge of the broad meaning of the term *value* contributes to the understanding of sustainability and its components as inherent values of the add-on service proposal. The philosophy underlying this consideration is the conception of values as moral and ethical precepts that underpin human behavior and their integral connection with education, culture, and experience, as well as with the place and time of their exercise. In short, value is commonly part of a value system that guides people's behavioral preferences in all situations.

The essence of sustainability in the service, including its industrial origin of manufacture, is in the optimal use of physical and nonphysical resources involved in the process and in attention to their categories of reduction, reuse, recycling, recovery, or regeneration to achieve efficient performance in the environmental, social, and economic dimensions of its composition.

(a) **The environmental value:** It is the option of adding value to the service, based on the maintenance and conservation of the ecosystem and biodiversity through the efficient use of the tangible resources involved in the process and the anticipation or control of its polluting effects.

(b) **The social value:** It is the option of adding value to the service by including social elements related to changes and positive impacts on the experiences and daily life of users and society in general with the service. The health, education, and welfare services, among others, are aimed at the provision of *social values*.

(c) **The economic value:** Generally referred to the price. However, the price of a product or service quantifies a wide range of factors whose value is still not entirely clear and which has given rise to many valuation methods and strategies. Among the price considerations are mainly the user/consumer, their needs, expectations, habits, social stratum, and so on, where it is necessary to distinguish between cost and value as well as *exchange value* and *value in use*. Consequently, the profitability of a product or service is associated with the satisfaction and loyalty of the consumer/user whose purchase decision is guided by the perceived value and the value in use of their experience with the product or service.

The process of evaluating physical resources to make a rational use of them in the established dimensions has given rise to the technique of "product life cycle analysis."[14, 15] The analysis starts from the extraction and processing of the raw materials that are used in the second phase of its manufacture. It continues with the third delivery phase that leads to its use where it should be kept or returned to the cycle for reuse or recycling, or concludes the life cycle with its disposal.

In this section, it is worth mentioning that the idea of the *circular economy* or restorative model emerges from the environment of sustainability and environmental quality, which gives foundation to the PAAS/PSS model indicated at the beginning of this chapter. A paradigm on the rise and alternative to the traditional linear economic model in three steps: *take-do-discard*.

From sustainability, service provision involves not only socio-environmental awareness or mentality but also the efficient use of tangible resources and the anticipation or reduction of their possible polluting effects. The product life cycle analysis scheme contributes to this purpose to identify and consider the treatment of these dimensions:

1. Describe the life cycle of the service with respect to the tangible resources used
2. Analyze and evaluate the inclusion, use, and disuse of the resource in each step of the process:
   (a) Collect information and direct and indirect data: polluting resources, facilities, landfills, and wastes.
   (b) Establish key performance indicators.
   (c) Identify the steps of the cycle with the greatest use of resources and polluting emissions.
3. Seek clean services and technologies that prevent, reduce, or replace, or increase the efficiency of the resource at each step.
   (a) Identify the steps of the process where the addition of services or clean technologies has the relevant potential for improvement.
   (b) Find the appropriate clean technologies and/or services.
   (c) Identify the limitations or restrictions for its implementation.
   (d) Identify the relevant indicators and compare with the possible alternatives.

These principles and approaches to sustainable development, conceived in the ecosystem of the service and integrated into the servitization process, add value beyond the scope of the service itself by inherently contributing to the social well-being and the conservation of natura_ and artificial ecosystems.

Application Exercise

Sustainability Strategies in Service

Objective

Strengthen knowledge and develop skills to identify resources and polluting impacts in service and apply strategies for their prevention, reduction or replacement, and increase of its efficiency.

Instructions

Applying the product life cycle analysis scheme:

(a) Describe the life cycle of a service (service journey map) of your interest from the perspective of the tangible resources used.
(b) Identify tangible resources, their polluting impacts, and efficiencies.
(c) Define strategies to prevent, reduce or replace, and increase their efficiency.
(d) Identify the limitations or restrictions for its implementation.
(e) Identify the relevant indicators.

Outcome

Appropriation of knowledge on sustainability and development of capabilities for identification resources and pollution impacts as well as strategy design and application in services provision.

Final Acknowledgment

Upon completing this application exercise, the reader will have acquired sufficient knowledge about the sustainability concept and managerial capabilities to provide services in an environmentally secure manner.

Appendix

Application Exercise

Design of a Servitization Strategy

Purpose

The following application exercise seeks to integrate in a practical way the knowledge, methods, and tools indicated in this work to strengthen the possible learning and its subsequent use in academic, business, and entrepreneurial contexts. This exercise consists of two phases:

1. Identification, analysis, and design of a service business opportunity based on Chapter 2: *Servitization: An Assessment Holistic Perspective.*
2. Design of the service proposal for adding value to the business applying the knowledge contained in Chapter 1: *The Service Value Chain.*

Outcome

Design project of a servitization strategy.

General Guidelines

Considering the categories (23) of *Manufacturing Industries* contained in the International Standard Industrial Classification of all economic activities (ISIC) of the United Nations that are indicated in Table A.1.

Table A.1 ISIC manufacturing industries

Category	Product
1	Preparation of food products
2	Preparation of beverages
3	Manufacture of tobacco products
4	Manufacture of textile products
5	Manufacture of clothing
6	Manufacture of leather products and related products
7	Wood production and manufacture of wood and cork products, except furniture; manufacture of articles of straw and plaiting materials
8	Manufacture of paper and paper products
9	Printing and playback of recordings
10	Manufacture of coke and refined petroleum products
11	Manufacture of chemical substances and products
12	Manufacture of pharmaceutical products, medicinal chemical substances, and botanical products for pharmaceutical use
13	Manufacture of rubber and plastic products
14	Manufacture of base metals
15	Manufacture of fabricated metal products, except machinery and equipment
16	Manufacture of computer, electronic, and optical products
17	Manufacture of electrical equipment
18	Manufacture of machinery and equipment n.e.c.
19	Manufacture of motor vehicles, trailers, and semitrailers
20	Manufacture of other types of transport equipment
21	Furniture manufacturing
22	Other manufacturing industries

Source: UN. 2009. International Standard Industrial Classification of All Economic Activities (ISIC), Rev.4, Statistical Papers (Ser. M), New York, NY: UN.

Part 1

Select from the previous list, an economic activity of your interest to design a servitization strategy and apply the *holistic valuation perspective*, described in Chapter 2 and formatted below:

1. **Motivation for the adoption of the servitization strategy. Previous analysis of organizational values and personal beliefs.**
   What value will the service bring to my business?
   What is the managerial attitude of adding a service environment to the business?

2. **Valuation perspective.** Identify in the selected economic activity the integral value chain of the business (valuation tree) and, from the principles and valuation criteria, define the corresponding categories of productive activities following the top-down method.

   NOTE: In this part of the application exercise, the case of the pharmaceutical industry described in Chapter 2 could serve as guidance and support.

3. **Service Business Opportunity.** Analyze the service option identified in the previous step and substantiate the business opportunity focusing attention on (a) the end user and (b) the market opportunity following the next steps:

   (a) End user:
   - Needs and expectations (tastes and preferences)
   - Market inefficiencies (quality of service)
   - Market players (competitors)
   - Market size and purchasing power (sufficiency)

   (b) Market opportunity:
   - The service proposal (attractiveness and added value)
   - Resources required (availability)
   - Financial feasibility (indicators)
     - Net present value (NPV)
     - Internal rate of return (IRR)
   - EBITDA

4. **Adoption decision.** Analyze the service business opportunity proposal defined in the previous point, determine the possible functional areas of the organization with which to consult and agree on the proposal before making the addition decision, and include it in the strategic objectives of the company for the resource allocation and implementation.

Part 2

Design the service proposal identified, reconciled and adopted in phase 1 and 3 on the content: The Systematic and Transversal Service of Chapter 1, both following the strategic vision of the service scheme of the business model:

1. The target market
2. Service proposal

3. Strategy
4. Delivery system
5. Compliance management

Final Acknowledgment

Upon completing this application exercise, the reader will have appropriated the knowledge, processes, and procedures covered in this work and required for the design and development of a servitization strategy. You will have a preliminary project to refine and agree on for consideration as a strategic objective of a company, and you will have fulfilled the purpose of this professional and academic experience.

Terminology

Differentiation (Marketing)

The unique, original, and novel character to differentiate or distinguish a product or service from those that exist in the market.

Patenting

Action to patent an industrial property.

Personal Service (Voluntary)

The action of freely giving and accepting to satisfy human needs, which results in the common benefit.

Polysemic

Linguistic expression to denote plurality of meanings.

Positioning (Marketing)

The placement of trademarks (distinctive signs) by companies in the marketplace as well as in the collective imaginary (mind) of consumers.

Praxeology

Study of the logical structure of conscious human action (praxis) in an aprioristic way.

Private Service (Exchange)

Provided for profit or remuneration by delegated private and public companies and corporations with the purpose of satisfying the particular needs and expectations of users/customers.

Public Service (Collaborative)

Services reserved, provided, and delegated by the public administration (government) as required by law to respond to the social activity.

Service

The action of co-creating value.

Service System

The integration, configuration, and dynamic alignment of resources of various kinds (human, financial, technological, infrastructures, information, etc.) in order to create shared value.

Servilogy

Study of the principles, concepts, approaches, methods, and instruments of service from the perspective of human action as a reasoned and deliberative behavior.

Service Design

The process of creation and development, comprehensive and effective, of the service proposal. The holistic view of the value-creation interaction in the user experience.

Service Delivery

The comprehensive and specific process of interaction, provision, and assurance of the appropriate use of the service.

Service Ecosystem

The set of entities that act in domain-specific roles as providers and users of services; of available services that enable community interaction and co-creation; and the appropriate architecture for engineering, delivery, and governance.

Service Engineering

The application of the knowledge generated by science for the creation of value and the construction of the capacity to provide the service.

Servimetry

The process of analysis and application of principles, knowledge, methodologies, and tools to measure the management and performance of the service and the relationship with the user/customer.

Service Taxonomy

Classification of the service by its etymological, morphological, and economic conception.

Servitization (Servicialization)

A strategic model or process of organizational innovation/transformation of co-creation of value for the business/manufacturing company through the identification and development of service opportunities.

Sustainable Service

The interaction process to satisfy the needs and expectations of the user, remaining innovatively in time without negatively impacting the natural or social environment.

Transversality

Transversal quality (that it intersects in a perpendicular direction with the thing in question).

Notes

Chapter 1

1. Von Mises (1998).
2. Ajzen and Fishbein (1980).
3. Kohtamäki, Baines, Rabetino, and Bigdeli (2018).
4. Maglio, Kieliszewski, and Spohrer (2010), p. 1.
5. Zeithaml, Bitner, and Gremler (2018).
6. Bordoloi, Fitzsimmons, and Fitzsimmons (2018).
7. Schmenner (1986), p. 25.
8. Vargas and Campos (2016).
9. Talbott (2006), pp. 6–13.
10. Bordoloi, Fitzsimmons, and Fitzsimmons (2018).
11. Maglio, Kieliszewski, and Spohrer (2010), p. 1.
12. Stickdorn, Hormess, Lawrence, and Schneider (2018).
13. Jacobides, Cennamo, and Gawer (2018), pp. 2255–2276.
14. Lusch and Vargo (2014).
15. Adner (2006), pp. 98–107.
16. Schmenner (1986), p. 25.
17. UN (2009).
18. WIPO (2021).
19. UN (2009).
20. WIPO (2021),
21. Heskett, Sasser, and Schlesinger (1997).

Chapter 2

1. Schulman, Dunleavy, Harmer, and Lusk (1999).
2. Kohtamäki, Baines, Rabetino, and Bigdeli (2018).
3. Vandermerwe and Rada (1988), pp. 314–324.
4. Frank, Mendes, Ayala, and Ghezzi (2019), pp. 341–351.

5. Palo, Åkesson, and Löfberg (2019), pp. 486–496.

6. Adrodegari and Saccani (2017), pp. 57–83.

7. Erguido, Marquez, Castellano, Parlikad, and Izquierdo (2019).

8. Annarelli, Battistella, Borgianni, and Nonino (2018), pp. 74–85.

9. Richter, Schoblik, Kölmel, and Bulander (2018), pp. 65–95.

10. Vaittinen, Nenonen, and Story (2019), pp. 139–159.

11. Lusch and Vargo (2004), pp. 1–17.

12. Fliess and Lexutt (2019), pp. 58–75.

13. Porter (1998).

14. Rajala, Brax, Virtanen, and Salonen (2019), pp. 630–657.

15. Porter (1998), p. 36.

16. Baines, Lightfoot, and Smart (2011), pp. 947–954.

17. Schmenner (2009), pp. 431–443.

18. Heskett, Sasser, and Schlesinger (1997).

19. Maglio, Kieliszewski, and Spohrer (2010).

20. Baines,Bigledi, Bustinza, Victor, Baldwin, and Ridgway (2017), pp. 256–278.

21. UN (2009).

22. The Coca cola company (2021); Apple Inc (2021); Inditex (2021); Rolls-Royce motor cars (2021); Aston University (2021); Caterpillar Inc (2021); Xerox (2021); Emerald publishing (2020).

Chapter 3

1. Parasuraman, Ziethaml, and Berry (1988), pp. 12–40.

2. Zeithaml, Parasuraman, and Malhotra (2005), pp. 213–233.

3. Kano, Seraku, Takahashi, and Tsuji (1984), pp. 39–48.

4. Reichheld (2006).

5. Blokdyk (2018).

6. Plutchik (1991).

7. Forrester Research Inc (2021).

Chapter 4

1. Martínez and Lázaro (2007), pp. 120–127.

2. Hefley and Murphy (2008).

3. Maglio, Kieliszewski, and Spohrer (2010).
4. The Institute of Customer Service (2002).
5. ICCSO (International Council of Customer Service Organizations) (2008).
6. Goleman (1998).

Chapter 5

1. Miles (1993), pp. 653–672.
2. Miles (2000), pp. 371–389.
3. Frank, Mendes, Ayala, and Ghezzi (2019), pp. 341–351.
4. Ayala, Paslauski, Ghezzi, and Frank (2017), pp. 9–18.
5. Schumpeter (1942).
6. Visnjic, Ringov, and Arts (2019), pp. 381–407.
7. Salonen, Saglam, and Hacklin (2017), pp. 662–686.
8. Forkmann, Henneberg, Witell, and Kindström (2017), pp. 275–291.
9. Kaplan and Norton (1996).
10. Gupta and Tyagi (2008).
11. Lusch and Vargo (2014).
12. Wolfson (2016).
13. Ibid.
14. Day (1981), pp. 60–67.
15. Finnveden, Hauschild, Guinée, Ekvall, Heijungs, Hellwege, Koehlere, Pennington, and Suhg (2009), pp. 1–21.

References

General

Benedettini, O., A. Neely, and M. Swink. 2015. "Why Do Servitized Firms Fail? A Risk-Based Explanation." *International Journal of Operations & Production Management* 35, no. 6, pp. 946–979.

Bordoloi, S., J. Fitzsimmons, and M. Fitzsimmons. 2018. *Service Management, Operations, Strategy, Information Technology*, 9th ed. McGraw-Hill Education.

Carlzon, J. 1989. *Moments of Truth, New Strategies for Today's Customer-Driven Economy.* Ballinger Publishing. New York, NY: Harper & Row.

Chalal, M., X. Boucher, and G. Marques. 2015. "Decision Support System for Servitization of Industrial SMEs: A Modelling and Simulation Approach." *Journal of Decision Systems* 24, no. 4, pp. 355–382.

Dahmani, S., X. Boucher, and S. Peillon. 2016. "A Reliability Diagnosis to Support Servitization Decision-Making Process." *Journal of Manufacturing Technology Management* 27, no. 4, pp. 502–534.

Lovelock, C., J. Reynoso, G. D'Andrea, and L. Huete. 2011. *Administración De Servicios, Estrategias De Marketing, Operaciones Y Recursos Humanos.* Pearson Education.

Maglio, P., C. Kieliszewski, and J. Spohrer, J. (editors). 2010. *Handbook of Service Science.* Springer.

Sousa, R. and G.J.C. da Silveira. 2019. "The Relationship Between Servitization and Product Customization Strategies." *International Journal of Operations and Production Management* 39, no. 3, pp. 454–474.

Van Bon, J., (Editor), A. de Jong, A. Kolthof, M. Pieper, R. Tjassing, A. Van der Veen, and T. Verheijen. 2010. *Fundamentos de ITIL 3.* Zaltbommel, The Netherlands: Van Haren Publishing.

Vandermerwe, S. and J. Rada. 1988. "Servitization of Business: Adding Value by Adding Services." *European Management Journal* 6, no. 4, pp. 314–324.

Von Mises, L. 1998. *Human Action: A Treatise on Economics.* The Ludwig von Mises Institute, AL, USA.

Weeks, R. and S. Benade. 2015. *The Development of a Generic Servitization Systems Framework Technology in Society* 43, pp. 97–104.

Zeithaml, V.A., M.J. Bitner, and D. Gremler. 2018. *Services Marketing: Integrating Customer Focus Across the Firm,* 7th ed. McGraw-Hill Education.

Specific

Adner, R. 2006. *Match Your Innovation Strategy to Your Innovation Ecosystem* 84, pp. 98–107. Harvard Business Review.

Adrodegari, F. and N. Saccani. 2017. "Business Models for the Service Transformation of Industrial Firms." *Service Industries Journal* 37, no. 1, pp. 57–83.

Ajzen, I. and M. Fishbein. 1980. *Understanding Attitudes and Predicting Social Behavior.* Prentice-Hall.

Annarelli, A., C. Battistella, Y. Borgianni, and F. Nonino. 2018. "Estimating the Value of Servitization: A Non-Monetary Method Based on Forecasted Competitive Advantage." *Journal of Cleaner Production* 200, pp. 74–85.

Apple Inc. 2021. www.apple.com.

Aston University. 2021. www.aston.ac.uk/.

Ayala N.F., C.A. Paslauski, A. Ghezzi, and A.G. Frank. 2017. "Knowledge Sharing Dynamics in Service Suppliers' Involvement for Servitization of Manufacturing Companies." *International Journal of Production Economics* 192, pp. 9–18.

Baines, T., A.Z. Bigdeli, O.F. Bustinza, G.S, Victor, J. Baldwin, and K. Ridgway. 2017. "Servitization: Revisiting the State-of-the-art and Research Priorities." *International Journal of Operations & Production Management* 37, no. 2, pp. 256–278.

Baines, T., H. Lightfoot, and P. Smart. 2011. "Servitization Within Manufacturing: Exploring the Provision of Advanced Services and Their Impact on Vertical Integration." *Journal of Manufacturing Technology Management* 22, no. 7, pp. 947–954.

Blokdyk, G. 2018. *Customer Effort Score, A Complete Guide.* 5STARCooks.

Bordoloi, S., J. Fitzsimmons, and M. Fitzsimmons. 2018. *Service Management, Operations, Strategy, Information Technology*, 9th ed. McGraw-Hill Education.

Caterpillar Inc. 2021. www.caterpillar.com/.

Day, G.S. 1981. "The Product Life Cycle: Analysis and Applications Issues." *Journal of Marketing* 45, no. 4, pp. 60–67.

Emerald publishing. 2020. *Servitization Case Studies.* www.emeraldgroup publishing.com/opinion-and-blog/what-servitization-manufacturing-a-quick-introduction8/2021.

Erguido, A., A.C. Marquez, E. Castellano, A.K. Parlikad, and J. Izquierdo. 2019. *Asset Management Framework and Tools for Facing Challenges in the Adoption of Product-Service Systems.* IEEE Transactions on Engineering Management.

Finnveden, G., M.Z. Hauschild, E.J. Guinée, T. Ekvall, R. Heijungs, S. Hellwege, A. Koehlere, D. Pennington, and S. Suhg. 2009. "Recent Developments in Life Cycle Assessment." *Journal of Environmental Management* 91, no. 1, pp. 1–21.

Fliess, S. and E. Lexutt. 2019. "How to Be Successful With Servitization–Guidelines for Research and Management." *Industrial Marketing Management* 78, pp. 58–75.

Forkmann S., S.C. Henneberg, L. Witell, and D. Kindström. 2017. "Driver Configurations for Successful Service Infusion." *Journal of Service Research* 20, no. 3, pp. 275–291.

Forrester Research Inc. 2021. *Customer Experience Index (CX Index).* www .forrester.com/blogs/category/customer-experience-index-cx-index/8/2021.

Frank, A., G.H.S. Mendes, N.F. Ayala, and A. Ghezzi. 2019. *Servitization and Industry 4.0 Convergence in the Digital Transformation of Product Firms: A Business Model Innovation Perspective, Technological Forecasting and Social Change* V, no. 141, pp. 341–351.

Goleman, D. 1998. *Working With Emotional Intelligence.* Batam Dell.

Gupta, P.K. and R.K. Tyagi. 2008. *Complete and Balanced Service Scorecard, A: Creating Value Through Sustained Performance Improvement.* FT Press.

Hefley, B. and W. Murphy. (Eds.). 2008. *Service Science, Management and Engineering: Education for the 21st Century.* US: Springer.

Heskett, J., W. Sasser, and L. Schlesinger. 1997. *The Service Profit Chain.* NY: The Free Press.

ICCSO (International Council of Customer Service Organizations). 2008. *International Customer Service Standards (ICSS).* Australia. www.iccso.org (accessed August 2021).

Inditex. 2021. www.inditex.com and www.expansion.com.

Jacobides, M.G., C. Cennamo, and A. Gawer. 2018. "Towards a Theory of Ecosystems." *Strategic Management Journal* 39, no. 8, pp. 2255–2276.

Kano, N., N. Seraku, F. Takahashi, and S. Tsuji. 1984. "Attractive Quality and Must-Be Quality." *Hinshitsu: The Journal of the Japanese Society for Quality Control* 14, no. 2, pp. 39–48.

Kaplan, R.S. and D.P. Norton. 1996. *The Balanced Scorecard.* Harvard Business School Press.

Kohtamäki, M., T. Baines, R. Rabetino, and A.Z. Bigdeli. 2018. *Practices and Tools for Servitization, Managing Service Transition.* Springer International Publishing, Switzerland: Palgrave Macmillan.

Lusch, R.F. and S.L. Vargo. 2004. "Evolving to a New Dominant Logic for Marketing." *Journal of marketing* 68, no. 1, pp. 1–17.

Lusch, R.F. and S.L. Vargo. 2014. *Service-Dominant Logic: Premises, Perspectives, Possibilities.* Cambridge University Press.

Maglio, P., C. Kieliszewski, and J. Spohrer. (Editors). 2010. *Handbook of Service Science*, p.1. Springer.

Martínez, Á. and P. Lázaro. 2007. *La Ciencia de los Servicios: un nuevo enfoque para la innovación en compañías de servicios*, no. 15, pp. 120–127. Universia Business Review.

Miles, I. 1993. "Services in the New Industrial Economy." *Futures* 25, no. 6, pp. 653–672.

Miles, I. 2000. "Services Innovation: Coming of Age in the Knowledge-Based Economy." *International Journal of Innovation Management* 4, no. 4, pp. 371–389.

Palo, T., M. Åkesson, and N. Löfbergb. 2019. "Servitization as Business Model Contestation: A Practice Approach." *Journal of Business Research* V, no. 104, pp. 486–496.

Parasuraman, A., V. Ziethaml, and L. Berry. 1988. "SERVQUAL: A Multiple-Item Scale for Measuring Consumer Perceptions of Service Quality." *Journal of Retailing* 62, no. 1, pp. 12–40.

Plutchik, R. 1991. *The Emotions*. University Press of America.

Porter, M.E. 1998. *Competitive Advantage: Creating and Sustaining Superior Performance*, Chapter 2, p. 36. NY: Free Press.

Rajala R., S.A. Brax, A. Virtanen, and A. Salonen. 2019. "The Next Phase in Servitization: Transforming Integrated Solutions Into Modular Solutions." *International Journal of Operations & Production Management* 39, no. 5, pp. 630–657.

Reichheld, F. 2006. *The Ultimate Question: Driving Good Profits and True Growth*. Harvard Business School Press.

Richter, A., J. Schoblik, B. Kölmel, and R. Bulander. 2018. "A Review of Influential Factors for Product Service System Application." *Revue Europeenne d' Economie et Management des Services* 1, no. 5, pp. 65–95.

Rolls-Royce motor cars. 2021. www.rolls-roycemotorcars.com/en_GB/inspiring-greatness/vision.html.

Salonen A., O. Saglam, and F. Hacklin. 2017. "Servitization as Reinforcement, Not Transformation." *Journal of Service Management* 28, no. 4, pp. 662–686.

Schmenner, R.W. 1986. "How Can Service Businesses Survive and Prosper." *Sloan Management Review* 27, no. 3, p. 25, Spring.

Schmenner, R.W. 2009. "Manufacturing, Service, and Their Integration: Some History and Theory." *International Journal of Operations & Production Management* 29, no. 5, pp. 431–443.

Schulman, D., J. Dunleavy, M. Harmer, and J. Lusk. 1999. *Shared Services: Adding Value to the Business Units*. John Wiley & Sons.

Schumpeter, J. 1942. *Capitalism, Socialism, and Democracy*. New York, NY: Harper & Bros.

Stickdorn, M., M.E. Hormess, A. Lawrence, and J. Schneider. 2018. *This Is Service Design Doing: Applying Service Design Thinking in the Real World*. Sebastopol, CA: O'Reilly Media.

Talbott, B.M. 2006. "The Power of Personal Service: Why It Matters What Makes It Possible How It Creates Competitive Advantage [Electronic Article]." *Cornell Hospitality Industry Perspectives* 1, no. 1, pp. 6–13.

The Coca cola company. 2021. www.coca-colacompany.com/company/purpose-and-vision.

The Institute of Customer Service. 2002. *National Occupational Standards in Customer Service at NVQ/SVQ Level 4.* U.K.

UN. 2009. *International Standard Industrial Classification of All Economic Activities (ISIC)*, Rev.4, Statistical Papers (Ser. M). New York, NY: UN.

Vaittinen, E., S. Nenonen, and V.M. Story. 2019. "Retailer Service Acceptance: Simply Adding a Service to the Offer Portfolio or Committing to Marketing It." *International Review of Retail Distribution and Consumer Research 2*, no. 2, pp. 139–159.

Vandermerwe, S. and J. Rada. 1988. "Servitization of Business: Adding Value by Adding Services." *European Management Journal 6*, no. 4, pp. 314–324.

Vargas, M. and A.X. Campos. 2016. *El Servicio en la Universidad de La Sabana.* Bogotá, Colombia: Dirección de publicaciones.

Visnjic, I., D. Ringov, and S. Arts. 2019. "Which Service? How Industry Conditions Shape Firms' Service Type Choices." *Journal of Product Innovation Management 36*, no. 3, pp. 381–407.

Von Mises, L. 1998. *Human Action. A Treatise on Economics*, The Ludwig von Mises Institute, AL, USA.

WIPO. 2021. The Nice Classification (NCL). https://www.wipo.int/about-wipo/en/8/2021.

Wolfson, A. 2016. *Sustainable Service.* ISSIP booklet, Business Expert Press. (Collections: Environmental and Social Sustainability for Business Advantage, Service Systems and Innovations for Business and Society, Digital Library).

Xerox. 2021. https://atyourservice.blogs.xerox.com/.

Zeithaml, V.A., A. Parasuraman, and A. Malhotra. 2005. "E-S-Qual: A Multiple-Item Scale for Assessing Electronic Service Quality." *Journal of Service Research 7*, no. 3, pp. 213–233.

Zeithaml, V.A., M.J. Bitner, and D. Gremler. 2018. *Services Marketing: Integrating Customer Focus Across the Firm*, 7th ed. McGraw-Hill Education.

About the Author

Strengthening the culture of service in the oil industry was the first contact with the servitization construct of **Antonio Pérez Márquez** when he assumed with his team of consultants-facilitators the design and execution of the corporate Service Management and Marketing Program as an organizational challenge to achieve the vision of "an energy corporation of world reference par excellence." In his book "Implosión Corporativa" (www.amazon.com), the scope and results of this business initiative are detailed.

The value of service in organizational performance was known by Pérez Márquez from training and practice from his management functions in the areas of human resources, marketing, and corporate communication in the oil sector; of its entrepreneurial initiatives of consulting and training in management and marketing of services (Instituto del Servicio al Cliente, Invermark Consultores y Soluciones CRM) in the manufacturing and services sectors; and its university teaching activities in recognized academies in the Latin American region: design, facilitation, and execution of projects, programs, and advanced degrees in Service Business Administration and Service Management and Engineering.

The specialized magazine "Contacto con el Cliente" served as an expression for Antonio Pérez Márquez to disseminate the events and advance the knowledge of the service, its practice, and results in the business field. His current academic and research activity on the subject make this edition possible and the subsequent transfer of research outcomes to industrial fields in the near future.

Index

Concise and Applied Business Books

The Collection listed above is one of 30 business subject collections that Business Expert Press has grown to make BEP a premiere publisher of print and digital books. Our concise and applied books are for…

- Professionals and Practitioners
- Faculty who adopt our books for courses
- Librarians who know that BEP's Digital Libraries are a unique way to offer students ebooks to download, not restricted with any digital rights management
- Executive Training Course Leaders
- Business Seminar Organizers

Business Expert Press books are for anyone who needs to dig deeper on business ideas, goals, and solutions to everyday problems. Whether one print book, one ebook, or buying a digital library of 110 ebooks, we remain the affordable and smart way to be business smart. For more information, please visit www.businessexpertpress.com, or contact sales@businessexpertpress.com.

www.ingramcontent.com/pod-product-compliance
Lightning Source LLC
Chambersburg PA
CBHW061830220326
41599CB00027B/5243